AF255731

The Beauty of God

The Beauty of God

Beauty, the Divine Attributes,
and the Life of Faith

BEN PUGH

CASCADE *Books* · Eugene, Oregon

THE BEAUTY OF GOD
Beauty, the Divine Attributes, and the Life of Faith

Cascade Books
An Imprint of Wipf and Stock Publishers
199 W. 8th Ave., Suite 3
Eugene, OR 97401

www.wipfandstock.com

PAPERBACK ISBN: 978-1-6667-5066-9
HARDCOVER ISBN: 978-1-6667-5067-6
EBOOK ISBN: 978-1-6667-5068-3

Cataloguing-in-Publication data:

Names: Pugh, Ben [author].

Title: The beauty of God : beauty, the divine attributes, and the life of faith / Ben Pugh.

Description: Eugene, OR: Cascade Books, 2023 | Includes bibliographical references.

Identifiers: ISBN 978-1-6667-5066-9 (paperback) | ISBN 978-1-6667-5067-6 (hardcover) | ISBN 978-1-6667-5068-3 (ebook)

Subjects: LCSH: God. (Christianity)—Attributes. | God—Beauty. | Theism. | Aesthetics—Religious aspects—Christianity.

Classification: BT130 P84 2023 (paperback) | BT130 (ebook)

02/06/23

Contents

Introduction

There can be few things more worthwhile than to study who God is. As our lives get caught up in peripheral things, this subject reminds us what matters, what ought always to be central. If the worship and service of God is the thing we were born for and will spend eternity doing, then surely the fuel for such a lifestyle of worship is an ever-growing appreciation for who God is.

Further, if our concern is that the image of God be restored in our soul: that we be healed of all the aspects of our character that have become misshapen by life's events, and by other damaged people damaging us, then what better way of restoring the image of God within us than to gaze upon the beauty of the Lord:

> One thing I asked of the LORD,
>   that will I seek after:
> to live in the house of the LORD
>   all the days of my life,
> to behold the beauty of the LORD,
>   and to inquire in his temple. (Ps 27:4)

Ultimately, this book has come into being as a result, not just of *loving* to gaze upon his beauty, but *needing* to. I came to faith from an unchurched background and throughout my childhood and adolescence I suffered a series of emotional knocks from bullying episodes, as well as years of isolation. By the time I came to faith I seemed to have acquired a few "demons." I probably don't mean actual demons, more that metaphorical kind that people like to mention when in autobiographical mode. What I mean is that for years after coming to faith at the age of nineteen, I struggled with what would today be described as mental ill health. Floating anxiety was especially persistent—that vague misgiving that refuses to tell its host exactly *what* the object of such fear is. And yet, occupying a neighboring place in my heart was a real fullness of the Holy Spirit and a passion for the Word of God. People commented on how full of God I seemed to be. I moved freely in the gifts of the Spirit and loved trying to be a friend to troubled people on the margins of church life.

I soon became a worship leader. I played a twelve-string guitar and could sing, and I learned all the latest *Songs of Fellowship* favorites that were doing the rounds of all the new charismatic networks. My earliest opportunities to lead worship were during a Tuesday night meeting of some forty young people that all met in the tiny front room of a retired soldier, Ashley, and his wife, Daphne. Ash and Daph were spiritual grandparents to us all. I soon discovered that seemingly everyone there was just like me: mostly unchurched and, in many cases, more messed up than I was. I was unwittingly part of a whole wave of young middle-class people coming to faith in the late '80s with little or no Christianity in their upbringings. Leading them all in worship, with a fellow art student playing the harmonica, was like touching heaven.

On the other days of the week I would worship the Lord for about an hour after coming home from college each night. I often had powerful experiences of his presence. I read in 2 Corinthians 3:18 that, if we keep gazing upon the glory of the Lord, we will be transformed into his likeness. I loved singing to him, but I also kept hoping that the happy by-product of this daily activity would be a fast-track to holiness. I hoped that this alone might be enough to transform me from one degree of glory to the next. I hoped I would hit the spiritual stratosphere of super-sainthood in no time at all. Truth is, there was probably something about the very desperation with which I wanted to change, something about the self-loathing of being a bullying survivor, that was itself in need of changing. I was yet to discover the wonders of justification—which is a whole other story.

So, this is just to set the scene. This is how gazing upon the beauty of the Lord came to be, and remains, so important to me, and how Psalm 27:4 ended up being an anchoring, guiding passage. I later studied theology to doctoral level and made a full-time career out of teaching people about God. Perhaps not surprisingly, a lecture called "The Attributes of God" has always been the lecture I most enjoy giving. There is always a strange hush that descends upon the room as the students have their minds opened by the Spirit to see glimpses of how great God is. I usually fail to get through every attribute. We have often stopped to offer thanks and praise to God. Before long, I even built in some praise-pauses. It seemed like the only way our minds could cope with such truths.

As it happens, my background in art has also meant that I was asked to help on a Creative Arts Mission and Ministry course. I often explored with my class what it meant to encounter God in the arts—and how Christian creatives might be able to produce work that is in some way owned by God. We all agreed that direct evangelism through the arts was not what we were about. My students would often share their frustrations about how their churches lacked appreciation for art. Anything less direct than a straightforward portrayal of a biblical scene or, even better, an embroidered biblical text, was viewed with suspicion or bewilderment, though this is starting to change. What was it, we asked, that might become an address from God to the viewer, the audience, the listener, the reader (we ambitiously tried to embrace all art forms)? Our conversations tended to revolve around two things: the transcendentals and the sacramental worldview. I encourage you to read on to find out more.

I have not structured this as a daily devotional, though each chapter could easily form part of a morning's devotions. There is usually a simple reflective question, and scriptural quotations tend to be given in full to save you the time involved in page flipping to each passage. And I encourage you to alight for a while on the very words of Scripture. I am not filling this book with Scripture quotes to pad it out, you understand. I think all my other books demonstrate that I can easily fill a book with my own words. But when it comes to describing God I have, again and again, come to the end of my words and have felt the need to give way to the Word of God. Please bear with me coming so soon to silence. It's me worshipping.

Summer 2022

Nottingham

1

On Beauty

THE GOOD, THE TRUE, and the beautiful are a once commonly used triad of concepts, inherited ultimately from Plato, that helped our ancestors understand what really mattered in life. The ultimate things of life, work, and relationships, the things that are never trivial, are so because they are good, true, and beautiful. These qualities are known as the "transcendentals" because they transcend every other way of classifying and understanding all that exists. Everything that exists is understood to be, to some extent, good, real, and beautiful. Every existing thing participates in these all-transcending qualities. Yet, many beings in the universe lack some of the goodness, truthfulness, and beauty they are supposed to display, and even the most beautiful thing cannot exhaust or define what beauty is. The same can be said for goodness and truth.

In art, much attention has naturally been given to this third transcendental: beauty. For many, it shares with goodness and truth the status of the ultimate ineffable reality behind every earthly form, and something that breathes itself mysteriously into a truly great artistic creation. It appears to be the touch of God himself, and the great icon painters of the Eastern tradition fully expected God to own their efforts as they humbly offered their artistic services to him.

We often experience God by being confronted in some way by beauty. Just as Dostoyevsky said: "Beauty will save the world."[1]

1. Dostoyevsky, *The Idiot*, 356.

It has been pointed out that the Greek word for beauty—*kalos*—is derived from the verb "to call." Beauty *summons* us, calls us into a world that is both beyond us and beyond the beautiful entity that we are encountering, whether it be a work of visual art, a piece of music, or the wonders of God's creation.

There is indeed an otherness about beauty—wherever it may be found—that has the power to redeem us. This was the reason why the psalmist wanted to behold the beauty of God (Ps 27:4). In the psalm, beholding the beauty of the Lord alludes to the *shekinah* glory of God that would appear in the tabernacle. Yet, the psalmist is clearly not literally expecting to see the glory of the Lord in the tabernacle he had set up since the glory would appear only within the most holy place on the day of Yom Kippur. Only the high priest was privy to this awesome event. Rather, the psalmist is describing a desire to take this priestly encounter with God into everyday life, to democratize and universalize the sacred so that it breaks through the secular (though, needless to say, the psalmist would not have thought about this in quite those terms). He wants unbroken communion with the Lord in *every* situation, and beauty is key to this aspiration. Without beauty, the psalmist's noble intention would fall flat on its face. But, when he sees the delightfulness and pleasantness of the Lord, what began as a service rendered *to* the Lord in devoted prayer and praise (like the priests in the tabernacle) becomes a "service rendered by God."[2] Beholding the beauty of God becomes "the means whereby God himself delivers man from the profane attitude of his mind and enables him to adopt a different attitude, an attitude determined by the experience and assurance of the nearness and reality of the Living God."[3]

Plato's Socrates describes the elevating power of contemplating beauty:

> And the true order of going, or being led by another, to
> the things of love, is to begin from the beauties of earth
> and mount upwards for the sake of that other beauty,

2. Weiser, *The Psalms*, 248.

3. Weiser, *The Psalms*, 249. Please forgive my use of this author's non-gender-inclusive language for humanity.

using these as steps only, and from one going on to two, and from two to all fair forms, and from fair forms to fair practices, and from fair practices to fair notions, until from fair notions he arrives at the notion of absolute beauty, and at last knows what the essence of beauty is.[4]

So, what is beauty? Both Plato and Aristotle attempted to define beauty as involving such properties as proportion, harmony, unity, order, symmetry, definiteness. Aquinas thought of it as involving integrity, proportion, and radiance. And not until the early modern era, did beauty become divorced from the other two transcendentals: goodness and truth. More recently, Balthasar sought to reintegrate them and in so doing expresses a wise guiding principle: "The beautiful guards the other transcendentals and sets the seal on them: there is nothing true or good, in the long term, without the light of grace of that which is freely bestowed."[5]

Jeremy Begbie points out how important it is, when we consider beauty, to distinguish it absolutely from sentimentality.[6] He rightly points out how it is possible for the same person to be intensely sentimental and yet shockingly cruel at the same time, giving the example of a camp commandant at Auschwitz who could weep at an opera performed by condemned Jewish prisoners. This fact, commonly played upon in films, is a truism that ought to alert us to the pathological nature of unbridled sentiment. It is the indulgence of the human emotions in feeling something for the pleasure of feeling it: feeling pity, for instance, yet taking no action at all to alleviate the suffering seen.

The Reformation and its famous disregard for visual forms of beauty helped to set the scene for a complete sea change in the Western aesthetic sense. Protestant churches, devoid of visual paraphernalia, actively encouraged the soul-searching journey within, as well as a new emphasis on the written Word. Creativity moved into literature and the stage play. Then came the Enlightenment.

---

4. Plato, *Symposium* 211c–d.

5. Balthasar, *Theological Aesthetics: Glory of the Lord*, 2:38.

6. Begbie, "Beauty, Sentimentality and the Arts," in Treier et al., eds., *The Beauty of God*, 45.

The scientific worldview began to make traditional ideas of beauty seem untenable. In place of the search for the harmony and oneness of things there was a quest for technological mastery.[7] During that era, Edmund Burke's work of 1757, *A Philosophical Inquiry into the Origins of Our Ideas of the Sublime and the Beautiful*, represented a significant break from the theological study of aesthetics. This new approach focused on the effect of the beautiful upon the senses. Balance, smoothness, delicacy, and color were all seen to primarily affect the senses—a shift that moves us closer to the idea of the appreciation of beauty as being mere pleasure, and not as meaningful as we had thought. Immanuel Kant (in his *Critique of Judgment* of 1790) insisted that the truly beautiful or artistic is, by definition, without inherent purpose and aesthetic judgments are, by definition, disinterested. It seems we do not delight in or desire a beautiful thing because of any functional quality that it has but simply because it is beautiful. Much later, modern and postmodern art would capitalize upon the new meaninglessness of aesthetics by producing art that deliberately made no reference to anything beyond itself. It was, effectively, meaningless in every sense other than the visual elements that make up a piece and how they interact to produce other visual phenomena. A piece of art could even be purely about the physical process that produced it, as with Jackson Pollock.

Beauty effectively ceased to be a transcendent, God-infused quality. Christianity tried to meet modernity on its own rationalistic terms by turning all its attention to demonstrating the good and the true in its message. And a Christianity that went along with modernity and subscribed merely to the true (faith as a system of correct propositions) or merely to the good (faith as that which is most morally good for people) would be, as far as Balthasar was concerned, a Christianity knocked down from its own heights.[8]

Meanwhile, art became less and less about beauty and more and more about truth: confronting the viewer with the horrible naked truth about ourselves. And, where music is about traveling through a rhythmic kind of time, momentarily delivering us from

---

7. Treier et al., eds., introduction to *The Beauty of God*, 8.

8. Balthasar, *Theological Aesthetics: Glory of the Lord*, 2:38.

our situatedness in space, the visual arts do the opposite. They stop time and make us forget it. Visual art forces viewers to concentrate on a point in space.[9] Hence, it is no surprise that those who have wanted to be provocative have gravitated to painting, sculpture, and installations. These, literally, stop us in our tracks. The result is often unedifying. Philip Ryken has even said, "In many ways the art world has become . . . a suburb of hell."[10] The Turner Prize has become notorious with the great many who feel that they are uninitiated into the world of ugly art and simply don't get it.

Ideally, beauty should work in perfect balance with goodness and truth. It interacts with goodness and truth by attracting us to them.[11] Beauty is a "spur to spiritual commitment," says Daniel Gustafsson. It is "that which pleases us without awakening our lust," and "the salt and sustenance of saints."[12] Beauty is on the threshold of the transcendental and the sacred, according to the late great Roger Scruton.[13] Beauty draws us by the power of gratitude for the sheer gift that is beauty.[14] "Beauty is there," says David Bentley Hart, "abroad in the order of things, given again and again in a way that defies description and denial with equal impertinence."[15] Like any free gift, beauty catches us by surprise. It is always startling, always seems to come from beyond, and points back to that other world from which it came more eloquently than the greatest sermon ever preached.

Perhaps surprisingly for a Puritan theologian, Jonathan Edwards was a great appreciator of the spiritual power of beauty:

> All the beauty to be found throughout the whole creation, is but the reflection of the diffused beams of that Being who hath an infinite fullness of brightness and

9. Dyrness, *Visual Faith*, 144.

10. Ryken, *Art for God's Sake*, 13: "Such artwork does not reveal the redemptive possibilities of a world that, although fallen, has been visited by God and is destined for his glory."

11. De Gruchy, *Christianity, Art and Transformation*, 104.

12. Gustafsson, "Beauty of Christian Art," 178.

13. See Scruton, *Beauty*.

14. Gustafsson, "Beauty of Christian Art," 180.

15. Hart, *Beauty of the Infinite*, 16.

glory; God . . . is the foundation and fountain of all being and all beauty.[16]

To behold beauty is to make proper use of a portal into the heavenly realm that God has littered his creation with. These portals are everywhere: both among the natural, the semi-natural, and the human-made entities of the earth. I have found beauty portals into God in everything from Ralph Vaughn Williams's *The Lark Ascending* to a summer night's walk along an old hedge in a field.

We can make a start in training ourselves to make more use these portals by studying who God is. Knowing what to look for in God will open our eyes to what he is doing and our ears to what he is saying through the mundane that surrounds us every day. Then, like the life that the psalmist aspired to, we may find that we are dwelling in the house of the Lord all the days of our lives.

> One thing I asked of the LORD,
> that will I seek after:
> to live in the house of the LORD
> all the days of my life,
> to behold the beauty of the LORD,
> and to inquire in his temple. (Ps 27:4)

16. Edwards, *Nature of True Virtue*, 125.

2

Self-Existence

This is the first of the "incommunicable" attributes. By "incommunicable" we don't mean that God doesn't tell us about them. He clearly does. "Incommunicable" in this case is the term that theologians use to refer to those aspects of God's nature that are *unique to God* and that humans (and other creatures) can never develop. They can't be transmitted to us, not even when we get to heaven. These are the attributes that make us gasp in wonder and we feel unable to fully understand them.

In short, these incommunicable qualities are the most fundamental reason why we worship. If God merely resembled us but was better than us in every way, we would probably like him a lot. He'd be quite the celebrity. In fact, if the present state of our culture is anything to go by, we'd like him so much we wouldn't be able to cope with it and so we'd be endlessly trying to dig up some dirt about him. But, with God, the option of liking him, or being jealous of him because he's better than us, is not open to us. God elicits an altogether different response. We *worship* him when we see that he is *not* like us, that he is altogether exalted.

God does have other qualities that are like ours, in fact, he gave those qualities to us, and we do feel great swells of gratitude toward him because of the kindness we see. And that kindness is like human kindness, but altogether better. But what makes us fall before him is his *unlikeness* to us. These super-exalted attributes are what the psalmists are referring to when they describe God as "great and most worthy of praise" (Ps 145:3) and as "exalted far above all gods" (Ps 97:9).

The fountainhead of these exalted qualities is what we call God's *self-existence*. By self-existence we mean that God's existence is something that he *owes only to himself*. Every other existing thing exists because it was brought into being, and remains held in being, by God. But he alone exists *independently*. Yet, as so often happens when we try to speak of who God is, language fails us. "Independently" in no way captures it, not even if we take our notion of human independence and magnify it as much as our minds will allow.

Building, then, on this idea of independence, which will have to suffice for now, we can say, for starters, that *God does not depend on anything outside of himself for his existence or sustenance.* Right now, I am feeling hungry because I want my breakfast. I'm looking forward to my porridge. And this need of things outside of myself for my sustenance is so normal, both for me and for everyone I know, that I hardly even question it. We are away in the Lake District in the North of England and I have left behind me a small menagerie of pet creatures that are even more highly dependent on things than I am. I have set up an automated humidifier and some long-lasting pots of special food for the gecko, I have left a block of holiday food for the fish. I have also left some blackberry wine fermenting and have placed a warming band around the fermenting bucket to ensure that the temperature will stay optimal for the yeast to be able to thrive. I also added a sachet of yeast nutrients. These are creatures so small I cannot even see them, yet I am aware that they too have needs. Dependence upon outside help is a fact of life wherever we encounter it.

Not so for God, the Source of life itself.

God is the ground of existence. God brought every existing thing into being and so can never be referred to as though he were one of the things in the universe. He is *El Shaddai*, the *All*-Sufficient One, He Who Suffices (Gen 17:1).

Aristotle noted how everything in the universe is acted upon or is moved by something else. Those things, in turn, act upon other things. That's just the way things work. God, therefore, must,

Aristotle thought, be the "unmoved mover," the one who acts upon other things but who, uniquely, is never himself acted upon.[1] He moves other things but is himself never moved. Thomas Aquinas later argued, he is the first cause, himself uncaused.[2] Anyone who has had young children will be familiar with that phase they often go through at the age of two or three when they keep asking the question "Why?" If you allow a child to ask the "why" question for long enough then, according to Aquinas, you would reach the end of the line of explanations and be forced to simply say "because God."

God's self-existence is clearly expressed by the saying "I AM who I AM" (Exod 3:13–14). The divine name revealed in that passage could be rendered along the lines of "I will always be what I will always be." In the Greek translation known as the Septuagint it is translated as "I am the One who is."

Let's explore some of the ramifications of this. Firstly, God's self-existence, God's uncaused "I AM" nature, means that he has no needs. We have already established this, but here it is in the Scriptures: "If I were hungry I would not tell you . . . ," he says in Psalm 50:12, "for the world and all that is in it is mine." He famously owns "the cattle on a thousand hills." It is easy to see why the prosperity teachers like this verse, and they are not wrong to like it. It should indeed help us not to worry about God's provision when he is so rich! And here is Acts 17:25: ". . . nor is he served by human hands, as though he needed anything, since he himself gives all mortals life and breath and all things." The gods of the ancient world were quite needy. They got angry and vindictive if they were not placated with food and drink; they fell out with each other and murdered each other. The Greek myths are more like the lifestyles of the rich and famous, full of intrigue and stories of illicit affairs. Paul, in this last passage quoted, is explaining to the Athenians just how very far beneath God such behavior is. He is what divinity is *meant* to look like.

Secondly, God is independent in his reasoning and decision-making; no one ever gave God a good idea: Romans 11:34: "For

---

1. Discussed in Book XI of his *Metaphysics*.
2. Aquinas, *Summa Theologiae*, Prima Pars, Question 2, Article 3.

who has known the mind of the Lord? Or who has been his counsellor?" Indeed, there is nothing he owes us, no matter how well we have done, no matter how hard we think we have worked. He does not owe us success or applause: "Who has ever given to him, to receive a gift in return?" And the reason is his self-existence: "For from him and through him and for him are all things. To him be the glory forever. Amen" (Rom 11:35–36).

Thirdly, he needs no one's permission to do anything: "There is no one who can stay his hand or say to him, 'What are you doing?'" (Dan 4:35).

Finally, God is independent in the exercise of his power. He has the power to do whatever he wants, because, "our God is in the heavens; he does whatever he pleases" (Ps 115:3).

But let us go back to the all-important "I AM" moment of Exodus 3:14. It is probably no exaggeration to say that this moment kicks off a story within the story of the whole Hebrew Bible. From this moment, the underlying story it tells, and the theme it constantly returns to is, "Will the people of God worship the God-who-is or will they go after gods-who-are-not?" Will they worship the God who is all-sufficient and not made by human hands but has the ground of his existence within himself? Or will they prefer a woefully deficient and totally dependent thing that they have created and now call a god?

Here's what I mean by this great story within the story. The exodus story is a story of triumph over the *gods* of Egypt, not the people of Egypt, or even Pharaoh necessarily. The Ten Commandments begin with: "you shall have no other gods before me" (Exod 20:3). The story of the wilderness wanderings is a story of faithfulness to God and the covenant he had just inaugurated through Moses, versus the allure of other loyalties. The story of the conquest and settlement of Canaan is a story about a generation that had no memory of the great wonders that the God of Israel had performed, and that now faced the culture shock of a sedentary existence in which the skills of agriculture must be learned. They noted that the natives worshipped Baal to make the land fertile, so they did the same. The story of the monarchy is a story of monarchs who did what was right in the sight of the Lord by honoring and obeying him and monarchs who did what was evil by going after other gods and leading Israel astray in the same idolatry. The prophets are all aghast at how completely their own people had bowed down to gods of wood and stone that can be of no help at all. Proverbs, similarly, categorizes people as the wise and the foolish. The wise is the category of people who fear the Lord and are thus rewarded with a good life. The foolish are those who do not and who turn to idols. In the New Testament too, the specter of idolatry has not gone away. John warns against it (1 John 5:21); Paul warns against it (1 Cor 10:14), and it is no accident that the whole argument of Paul's classic work, the Letter to the Romans, begins with the assertion that humanity's primary problem is the fact that we have tended to worship the creature rather than the creator (Rom 1:18–23).

Could it be, then, that the mother or father all sins, the main problem we have, is *idolatry*? Bear in mind, too, that the Bible's main concept of worship is not necessarily acts of ceremony or singing. The word used is "follow." Israel is called upon to *follow* the Lord. Elijah asks the people gathered at Mount Carmel to choose whether they will follow the Lord or follow Baal (1 Kgs 18:21). Jesus' first recorded words to Peter, Andrew, and the two sons of Zebedee are "*follow* me" (Mark 1:16–20). This idea is also framed as "walking in his ways" (e.g., Ps 81:13), and the promise of the new covenant entailed the placing of God's Spirit inside his people so that they would be caused to walk according to his statutes (Ezek 36:27), echoed by Paul in Galatians 5:16 (NKJV): "Walk in the Spirit and you will not gratify the desires of the flesh." And what are those works of the flesh? Near the top of the list comes "idolatry" (Gal 5:20).

Are we following the God-who-is, the God who really is God, the all-sufficient I AM, or are we walking in the ways of gods that can be seen—and even controlled—but which, for that very reason, are no-gods? I think that our human nature is such that we much prefer gods of our own making. In a secular culture, the refusal to worship the true God continues. There is a taken-for-granted refusal to acknowledge him. And we share with the ancients a preference for the tangible over the intangible. Yet our forbears were more honest with themselves at this point. They shared with us a refusal to acknowledge the unseen and exalted God and they preferred things that are tangible and controllable, so they then went about crafting actual idols made of wood, stone, or metal. And they went ahead and bowed down to them. We, however, think such behavior is silly and pride ourselves on not being religious at all. We are neutral, secular entities.

The point I want to make is that the instinct to worship is so strong in us that, within the biblical perspective, that there is no neutral, worship-free ground where we can stand. We cannot simply opt out of religion and faith. From the divine viewpoint, we were created to worship, and we are, therefore, all engaged in it. For the "no religion" person in our culture, there may be no way, humanly speaking, that we can open their eyes to the fact that *they are already a worshipper*, a devotee of something or someone, but for the believer the situation is different. As believers we have already owned up to our worshipful instinct and, we hope, channeled it in the right direction.

Our problems come when disorder enters our worship. Somebody recently described addictions as a "worship disorder."[3] I like that phrase. It alerts us to what can go wrong in the life of faith. To begin with, the disorder seems to take the form of a coldness and dutiful ritualism in our hearts. We don't understand what has happened to our feelings for God but usually content ourselves with the thought that "it's not all about feelings," and double down on our disciplines because, we think, that's when faith really counts: when it's tough, when it's a "sacrifice of praise." Then, of course we find that, by being tough on ourselves we make matters worse still. It is in that moment of honesty that we realize we haven't grown cold at all. We haven't stopped being a passionate worshipper. It is simply that we have started passionately worshipping something else.

REFLECTION

Take a moment to be honest with yourself about worship. Are you only following, serving, worshipping the self-existing, all-sufficient

3. See Thomas, "Addiction Defined."

I AM, and going to him alone with *all* your needs? Or is your heart divided?

Or, maybe you are surrounded by people who all want a piece of you. Everyone makes a claim or demand upon you. No one is attending to *your* needs. Take time to lie back into the inexhaustible sufficiency of God's care. Curl up in the absorbent enveloping life of the living God.

3

Limitlessness

SPACE

THERE ARE THINGS WE know about and there are things we know nothing about. We know that the universe is vast beyond measure. Our earth can fit into the sun 1.3 million times, and our sun is of a relatively modest size compared to many of the other stars that fill the countless galaxies of stars that fill the known universe. What we still don't know is whether there is life on other planets. We are fairly sure there is no life on any of the planets within our solar system, but what about the four thousand planets that have so far been discovered within our galaxy alone?[1]

Spatially, we know of three dimensions: width, length, and depth, with time as a fourth. What we don't know about are the numerous other dimensions revealed by "string theory," each of which are probably infinitesimally small.[2]

There is a *lot* we don't know, some of which is potentially important knowledge about other life-forms and other dimensions of space-time. Yet, for all that, we are more prone than ever to commit the "epistemological fallacy." Epistemology is a term referring to what we know and how we come to know it. The epistemological

1. See NASA, "Is There Life on Other Planets?"
2. Try this: Daley, "We Haven't Been Zapped Out of Existence Yet."

fallacy describes what happens when we reach the limits of our competence at knowing. We reach the end of the epistemological line and conclude that nothing exists beyond it. We equate what *is* with what *can be known*. Absurd though this stance is, there is, in education theory for instance, an approach that is now so widespread it is an almost taken-for-granted assumption in university courses that train teachers how to teach. It is called "social constructivism." It is a theory founded on the conviction that knowledge is socially constructed. There is no truth or reality "out there" waiting to be discovered. We create our own truth, and socially we construct together a shared view of the world. And each world that a social group creates is just as valid as the next one. There is no "extra-mental" universe at all. There is nothing out there, only perspectives. What we know *is* what there is because what we know is only a construct.

It is as though the world has developed a mystery-phobia: a strong aversion to anything—anything outside of fiction, that is— that is not immediately explainable. And so, we conclude there is nothing out there at all, just ideas, thoughts, values, stories, reactions, feelings, words. Nothing more.

If we think about it, the idea that there is really nothing "out there" at all except for humanly constructed knowledge is much more terrifying than the thought that there is a world out there, but it is full of things we don't know about yet. Breaking free of the epistemological fallacy involves admitting that most of reality is so vast and so complex that we have scarcely even begun to measure it or control it. In fact, these vast incomprehensible realities are probably in control of our lives far more than we can imagine.

As the modern age dawned and scientific knowledge of the cosmos increased, believers increasingly resorted to the "God of the gaps." In other words, wherever science reached its limits, such as in evolutionary missing links, believers stepped in and said, "There's God." In that little gap in scientific know-how, there he is, see? I think what I'm proposing here is the exact opposite of that. Human knowledge occupies those little hedges and ditches around the vast open fields of reality known only to God:

> Can you find out the deep things of God? Can you find
> out the limits of the Almighty? It is higher than the heav-
> en—what can you do? Deeper than Sheol—what can you
> know? Its measure is longer than the earth and broader
> than the sea. (Job 11:7–9)

God of the gaps? Hardly.

What has really happened is that our whole culture has become obsessed with the self. We are more obsessed than ever about
being ourselves, being authentic, being true to ourselves, and we are
less open than ever to the notion that there is a transcendent reality
"above" and "beyond" us. We have flattened out reality to the tame,
banal dimensions that we know about.

Even after building a magnificent temple for God, Solomon
admitted: "Even heaven and the highest heaven cannot contain
you, much less this house that I have built" (1 Kgs 8:27). God is not
confinable within our space. He is not even limited to the universe.

We can be tempted to ask, "Why would such an immense God
care about me?" The wonder of the Hebrew Bible is that it keeps
in perfect balance, like no other writing I know, God the highly
exalted one *and* God the ever-present one. His transcendence is
balanced by his immanence:

> Where can I go from your Spirit? Or where can I flee
> from your presence? If I ascend to heaven, you are there.
> If I take the wings of the morning and settle on the far-
> thest limits of the sea, even there your hand shall lead
> me, and your right hand shall hold me fast. (Ps 139:7–10)

The Reformed theologian Louis Berkhof tries to capture this
balance of transcendence and immanence: "He transcends all spa-
tial limitations, and yet is present in every point of space with the
whole of His Being."[3] God is not spread out everywhere, with one
part of God here and another part of him there. Rather, God is everywhere present *with the whole of himself.*

---

3. Berkhof, *Systematic Theology*, 60.

REFLECTION

God is not too busy for you. He is not aloof. He is vast enough to be intimately involved with you. Whatever you face, you will never face it alone. Conversely, whatever you want to do in secret, you cannot tell God to close his eyes. He can be an uncomfortable companion to have around.

The good news is that he does not wish to be just theoretically present. Isaiah, speaking for God, did not say, "Fear not for I am omnipresent, filling every point of space with the whole of my being," he said, "Fear not, for I am *with you*" (Isa 41:10). The very fact that God is a Trinity—in other words, the fact that he exists as a set of relationships—means that relationship is his approach to everything. If he wants you to know he is present, he does this in a personal way. Because this is the case, he has a way of making his presence known to you in a way that is unique to you. We can miss this if we are always seeking experiences like the ones we hear described from the pulpits. Take time to reflect on how God has tended to make his presence known to *you*. How has he let *you* know he is there for you?

TIME

God's relationship with space, of course, is not the only way in which we must describe his infinity, since he also has a very peculiar relationship with time. He stands outside of both space and time. He is not subject to the limitations of that which he himself has authored. Just as with God's immensity, his eternity—his infinity in relation to time—is revealed in what we don't know. As the past disappears over the horizons of memory and as the future stubbornly refuses to reveal its secrets to us, there God dwells. He is there right now in all past events, ready to bring justice or healing in the present. And, whatever the future holds for us, he is there right now. He is already with us in those moments that for us are yet to be: rejoicing with us in the good times and carrying us through the bad.

God's transcendence of time is sometimes described as the "eternal now." The eternal now of God is described by Berkhof: "He is elevated above all temporal limits and all succession of moments and possesses the whole of His existence in one indivisible present."[4] Again, profound words worth pondering on. However, biblically, God's eternity is described not so much in terms of the eternal now, but more in terms of God's everlastingness: "From everlasting to everlasting you are God" (Ps 90:2). The biblical writers, while doubtless aware of the way God dwells outside of our time, seemed to find much more delight in the way God meets us *within* time. They spoke, not so much of his tim*eless*ness but of his tim*eful*ness.

If I were to enjoy a procession, I could either march and dance with the procession through the street, or I could take the elevator to the top floor of one of the highest buildings along the procession route and look down on it from above. If the building were tall enough, I could even see the end of the procession and its beginning. God, who sees the end from the beginning (Isa 46:10), who is the Alpha and Omega (Rev 21:6), prefers to dance with us. And when he does that, we are touched by eternity.

How does it feel to be touched by eternity? C. S. Lewis reckoned that those moments when we have so placed ourselves before God that the past is not bothering us and the future is not tyrannizing us, these moments are the closest thing to eternity that we experience in this life.[5]

Again, what does it feel like to be touched by God's eternal nature? It feels like renewal. Indeed, this is probably what revivals are: they are heaven touching earth. And when heaven touches earth, it comes to life. Flowing from God's eternal being is the new creation (2 Cor 5:17), the second birth (1 Pet 1:3–4), the making of all things new (Rev 21:5), the doing of a new thing (Isa 43:19), the renewal of the face of the earth (Ps 104:30). It is the *now* of God flooding the tirednesses and the passings away that seem to be the lot of this time-bound earth.

4. Berkhof, *Systematic Theology*, 60.

5. Lewis, *Screwtape Letters*, 75.

Retail therapy has a hold of us because it brings something very like this heaven-sent renewal. The things we already possess are forced to take one more step toward their eventual obsolescence, and, with the unboxing of the new thing, the future feels somehow redefined or given new possibilities. A stylish new outfit helps us to forget how unstylish our lowest moments have been and helps us picture ourselves in a better future, a going-places kind of a future. In this way, consumer culture gives us a pale and soon-fading simulation of the renewal of the Eternal Spirit. He it is that cleanses us of the past and revives our hearts to embrace his future.

REFLECTION

How do we tap into this heavenly renewal? "They that wait for the LORD will renew their strength" (Isa 40:31). We still our time as much as we can, in order to enter God's now, his timefullness. Then, God's now fills our present moment with newness: the renewal of our minds (Rom 12:3), the renewal of our inner morality (Col 3:10), and the renewal of our strength (Eph 4:23). And we arise from such a moment to find the past cleansed and the future redefined.

May the God who renews the face of the earth (Ps 104:30) send his Spirit to renew your life before him now.

4

Changelessness

Flowing logically from God's self-existence we discover, as we saw, his infinity. The self-existing creator of every existing thing cannot himself be bound by the time and space of the cosmos he founded. His infinity in relation to time we call eternity. And now, flowing logically from God's eternal nature comes the realization that he *does not change*. The eternity he dwells in is a *changeless* eternity because it is not subject to the succession of moments in which changes happen.

Also, because of his absolute self-sufficiency, he cannot be improved upon. All change involves either improvement or deterioration. You and I are always changing. It is a fact of life. What matters is whether we are getting worse or better. Staying the same is an option we will never get to choose. We are always being acted upon by other things in God's universe, and these factors cause us to get better or worse, whether physically, psychologically, or spiritually. As the absolute definition of perfection, God is incapable of either growing or declining.

Later we will see another thing he cannot do: he cannot lie. But here we ponder the more general fact that he cannot change. Now it is true that there are times in the Bible when God "relents" or seems to change his mind about something (e.g., Exod 32:9–14; Jonah 1:2; 3:4, 10), yet this is when human beings change, for example in repentance, and God displays a different shade to his unchanging character in response. God's ultimate plans and purposes remain unaffected.

For the life of faith, the first effect of encountering God's immutability (his attribute of being changeless) is that it makes us freshly aware of the earthly things we are clinging to: "They [the heavens and the earth] will perish, but you endure; they will all wear out like a garment. You change them like clothing, and they pass away; but you are the same, your years have no end" (Ps 102:26–27). At first, getting free of the hold that perishable things have over us feels painful, like being stripped of a favorite blanket. But then we taste the far better comforts of dwelling under the shadow of the Almighty (Ps 91:1), the fullness of joy in his presence and the pleasures that are at his right hand forever more (Ps 16:11). We know this, of course, but there are times when our flesh has taken over. It has made us into a seething knot of wriggling passions and slippery appetites, and it is time to detach ourselves from the earthly things that stir them.

These things will all pass away. Nothing will remain: not even success or fame; neither qualifications, nor titles, nor skill sets, neither our own good looks and athletic bodies, nor the handsome features of others to whom we might feel attracted; neither the noble nor the base among the world's allurements: nothing. And to cling to these things will make fools of us in the end.

The second effect of encountering the divine immutability is that we see God's dependability. I have sometimes been referred to by people as a "rock." I seem to level out their ups and downs, lifting them when they are down (at least, I try to!) and calming them when they are pumped, whether with panic or with joy. I compensate for their unreliability, I take any knocks when they need someone to lash out at, and I come across as only mildly impressed when they do well, despite my efforts at *trying* to be more demonstrative. I seem to keep people on an even keel. But this only really means that I am just a little less changeable than the people that come to me in need of my stability. But *even I* change. I am not the man I was twenty years ago, and, though my changes in mood may be less noticeable than many people's, I share with all humanity the capacity to feel happier or sadder, livelier or more lethargic, agitated or at peace. I change, but God is the *true* Rock.

God's changelessness means that, when we go to him, we can expect him to be the Rock of Ages, the Rock of rocks. He is the Rock whose work is perfect and whose ways are always just (Deut 32:4), a Rock in which we find refuge from the enemy (Pss 18:2; 61:2; 62:2, 6, 7; 71:3; 89:26; 94:22), or like a rock beneath our feet (Ps 27:5). He is the Rock we can always call upon (Ps 28:1) and be brutally honest with (Ps 42:9).

People have a way of turning out not to be what they were, or at least not what we thought they were, but God is never other than himself. In the words of Anselm, "Thou art . . . so identical with Thyself, that in no respect art Thou unlike Thyself,"[1] which probably sounds more profound than it is! God is always consistent, and if our refuge is in him then the ups and downs of the people we share our lives with will not floor us.

But not only is God dependable in character: all the things he *says* have this same reliable, stable quality too. His advice will remain entirely consistent, his promises can be entirely relied upon, and what he says he is doing is what he is *in fact* doing. Further, who he says he is, really is who *in fact* he is, and who he says we are is who *in fact* we are:

> God is not a human being, that he should lie,
>> Or a mortal that he should change his mind.
> Has he promised, and will he not do it?
>> Has he spoken, and will he not fulfil it?
> See, I received a command to bless;
>> He has blessed, and I cannot revoke it. (Num 23:19–20)

Has he promised you something? It will happen.

Has he said you are called to be this or that? Then, he has not changed his mind.

Has he said he will meet your need, then it does not matter how you may have failed, he will not fail you.

God's unchanging character means not only that he is a source of stability for us, and not only that everything he *says* is reliable

---

1. Anselm, *Proslogion* 18.

but also that everything he *does* is faithful—faithful to himself and faithful to us. He is *faithfully generous* (Jas 1:17), and *faithfully merciful* (Mal 3:6).

It also means that God's acts today closely resemble his acts in times past. J. I. Packer[2] was eager to point this out. Knowing that the God of the Bible is the same changeless one that we worship today is a source of comfort to us as we approach such a seemingly strange and distant book as the Bible. While it certainly helps us if we use good scholarship to bridge the immense historical and cultural gulf that separates our world from the biblical worlds, ultimately, what really makes this gulf bridgeable for us is the fact that the Spirit who inspired the words of Scripture is the very same Spirit who is with us and in us now. God today is *not other than* the God whom we meet in the Bible. And the writer to the Hebrews applies this truism to the second person of the Godhead: "Jesus Christ is the same yesterday and today and forever" (Heb 13:8). Was he working miracles in the Gospels? He is *not other than* that miracle-working God today. Was God defeating the powers of darkness in the pages of Scripture? Then that is the same God whom we cry out to today. Was he breathing his Spirit upon the church and making it effective in its mission in the book of Acts? That very same Spirit is upon us today, and, further, we are the *very same* church with the *very same* unchanging Christ as our Head.

There is, however, just one more sobering thought for us as we come to God in his marvelous immutability. We need to heed these wise words of A. W. Tozer:

> God will not compromise and He need not be coaxed. He cannot be persuaded to alter His Word nor talked into answering selfish prayer. In our efforts to find God, to please Him, to commune with Him, we should remember that all change must be on our part.[3]

Prayer involves us in the often-difficult process of changing shape *around* the changeless purposes of God for us, often through a painful series of disappointments. We thought we knew what

2. Packer, *Knowing God*, 83–85.

3. Tozer, *Knowledge of the Holy*, 75.

God wanted for us, but it turned out to be only what *we* wanted, and our feelings ran away with us. This is where our changeableness can be embraced as a gift rather than carried as a weakness. It is our very ability to change that makes us redeemable, sanctifiable: the kind of clay the unchanging, unfailing heavenly Potter loves to get to work on.

REFLECTION

So, God remains when all else perishes. He is the Rock of infinite reliability: constant in character, reliable in his words and consistent in his actions. He is not other than the God whom we meet in the Bible. It is, therefore, we, the changelings, who must use our malleability for good. As we go to God in prayer, it is *we* who must adapt, *we* who must change shape around this wonder-working Father, Son, and Spirit. Invite him to take your desires and transfigure them into his glorious purposes.

5

Singularity

It is stating the obvious, especially in view of the attributes we have so far considered, but there is a truth that the biblical writers state again and again: God is the *only* God. There is no other. There is none like him. There is nothing to compare to him. To use the language of the Olympic Games about transcending the category: God has transcended *every* category. This is the main meaning of the *Shema*, the creed of ancient Israel: "Hear O Israel: the Lord is our God, the Lord alone" (Deut 6:4).

The fact that he is the only true God implies several things:

HE IS TOTALLY OTHER

To express the otherness of God, the Bible tends to use words of altitude. There are some much-loved and much-sung passages. For example, he is "most high over all the earth," and "exalted far above all gods" (Ps 97:9). The name of the God of Israel is the "Most High" (e.g., Pss 7:17; 9:2; 92:1). The biblical worshippers also use the term "majesty" to express this absolute eminence: "The Lord reigns, he is clothed with majesty" (Ps 93:1). They speak of him as the most powerful monarch imaginable: someone whom you dare not approach without special permission.

In more modern times, this quality is expressed in Rudolf Otto's "overpoweringness."[1] God is *the* supreme being. Truly, he is "great" (Ps 48:1) and the only proper response is to "worship and bow down," and "kneel before the LORD our maker" (Ps 95:6). "For the LORD is great, and greatly to be praised; he is to be feared above all gods" (Ps 96:4).

Karl Barth was especially keen to point out that God is above and beyond our efforts to intellectually deduce what he is like. And we cannot reach him with our religiosity. We do not find God. God must find us; must disclose himself to us or else we end up worshiping a product of our own imagination. And, of course, worshipping a god of our own making has happened quite regularly throughout the history of the church, incurring the understandable derision of nonbelievers. The whole humanist project of Feuerbach and Comte was about writing off the Christianity they were familiar with as nothing but a projection: "The heaven of religion is nothing but a mirage in which man, uplifted by ignorance and faith, rediscovers his own image, but magnified and transposed—in other words, deified."[2] There may have been some truth in what they claimed. Maybe Christianity really had fallen from its worship of the one true God in deference to a God that can be liturgically tamed. Whatever the failure was, it created a space in which Comte's humanism could start the process, which is still going on, of assimilating and replacing all the unique claims of Christianity with its own God-free version of it.

Here's Karl Barth, writing to correct the idea that we can ever domesticate God:

> He is the One who stands above us and also above our
> highest and deepest feelings, strivings, intuitions, above
> the products, even the most sublime, of the human spirit.[3]

It is this transcendent otherness of God that produces in us a "shudder,"[4] a sense of holy fear when we sense his presence. It is the

1. Otto, *Idea of the Holy*, 20–23.
2. De Lubac, *Drama of Atheist Humanism*, 139–40.
3. Barth, *Dogmatics in Outline*, 37.
4. Otto, *Idea of the Holy*, 119.

experience that Otto describes as the "numinous," from the Latin "*numen*," which originally described the divine "nod," the expression of his will or consent. Later, the word came to mean any sense of the presence of divinity. Otto extends the idea even further to cover all experiences of the uncanny, including ghosts, but he stresses that the feeling reaches a unique intensity when we find ourselves face-to-face with God himself.[5] God's presence is a supremely powerful and holy presence. God, though filled with loving care beyond measure, awakens in us a sense of our "nothingness"[6] in comparison to him, filthiness in the light of him, and powerlessness to restrain or resist him. If we claim to know God but have never felt the numinous, never felt the terror, the power, the loftiness, then we may never have truly met him at all.

HE IS ENTIRELY UNIQUE

Isaiah, speaking for God and inspired by his Spirit, says, "To whom then will you liken God? Or what likeness will you compare to Him?" (Isa 40:18). Moses, straight after the closing of the Red Sea over the pursuing Egyptian army, is beside himself with wonder and awe: "Who is like You, O LORD, among the gods? Who is like You, glorious in holiness, fearful in praises, doing wonders?" (Exod 15:11).

This uniqueness of God extends to all his attributes and all his dealings with us. For example, in the case of his justice, it means that there is no higher court to which we can appeal. It is him whom we must fear, and him alone. He is the Judge of all, the Judge of judges, the Judge of human justice itself. But it also means that there is no one who loves like God does. His love cannot be compared to any earthly love, not even the highest of human loves. The greatest love poetry ever written cannot come close. Like the old hymn says, if the oceans were ink, the task of writing down what God's love is like would drain them.[7] It is a love that many a saint has found too

---

5. Otto, *Idea of the Holy*, 5–7.

6. Otto, *Idea of the Holy*, 10, 29, 91.

7. We will look at the hymn, "The Love of God," in chapter 10.

much to bear. Many have had to ask God to stay his hand lest they be entirely crushed by the intensity of it.

Indeed, everything that is true about God is uniquely so, and as such places him beyond the reach of language. Constant superlatives grow tired after a while, yet at the end of our finest words, there is still too much to say. Analogies are, of course, permitted, and we are his image-bearers so we do have at least a clue about what the Supreme Being logically *ought* to be like, and we will be resorting to these as we go on. But analogies and logical deductions are used with the proviso that they all crumble before his face when we meet him.

My faith journey began not with any prior idea about who God was that needed to be corrected, but with a direct encounter by which he showed himself to me. There was no religion in my upbringing. Both parents had understandably rejected the Churchianity of their upbringings by the time I came along one frosty January night in 1969. It all started in 1988 with vivid experiences of a presence. I had started having regular chats about Jesus with my friend in the student bar at art college. I always sensed a presence when we talked. It was as though the risen Jesus himself was at the table whenever we talked about him. I sensed him and knew that what I sensed was Jesus Christ. Then, at home in my student lodgings, a very similar presence would regularly light up the dreary surroundings of my room. It seemed like the room was being lit by a warm heavenly glow. The presence was a holy presence—so holy I quickly became aware of my unholiness. It was also a beautiful and tender presence, which clearly meant me no harm and planned only for my good. I have had countless experiences of the presence of God since then, each one slightly different, but these first encounters were enough to mean that my faith stayed firm for thirty years and more, down to the present day. One moment in the divine presence is still worth more to me than all the theology books I have ever read, and I never feel more alive than when I am lost in worship.

HE IS UNDIVIDED

There is just one more angle on the uniqueness of God that will be useful before we conclude, and that is "simplicity." Now, simplicity might seem like an odd word to use as we try to describe God, who is from one perspective incomprehensibly complex. But what is meant by simplicity, when we apply the term to God, is that *God is not a composite being*. For God to be made up of parts would necessitate substances that existed prior to or outside of him that were then somehow added together to make God, substances without which God cannot exist. In the union of humanity and divinity in Christ, there is a composition, but it is a composition that is *condescended to*. In Jesus of Nazareth, God took human flesh, but it is not essential to his being. "God is spirit" (John 4:24). The one who fills all things *chose* to assume a human nature. We, the creatures, have no choice but to be composed of the physical and the spiritual, the visible and the invisible. The disembodied state that we enter at the point of death, though blissful, is not complete. Completion will come, for us, with the resurrection of the body. The resurrection of Christ did not complete him, the Son of God is eternally complete. His resurrection signaled his victory over death on behalf of us.

REFLECTION

We serve a God who is far above all things and cannot be discovered by our intellection or religion. He is without comparison. There is no likeness that can survive the loving blast of his actuality. We meet God and are struck dumb. There is none like unto the Lord. Give him now your adoration. It is what you were created to do.

6

Knowledge

THIS IS THE FIRST of the "communicable attributes." By this we mean that these qualities, though supremely to be found in the divine being, are also part of our human nature. This is true of all the attributes that we will be considering from here on. As part of the "image of God" package that we were created with, all of us are endowed with these capacities, at least in some measure. The first of these are a threesome of attributes known as the intellectual attributes: knowledge, wisdom, and integrity (also known as truth or veracity). We begin with knowledge.

Human knowledge sometimes reaches extraordinary heights. Humans can hold the most enormous complexities in their heads and can perform the most extraordinary feats with their minds. The wonders of scientific, technological, and medical breakthroughs that we have seen in our lifetimes are traceable to that vast unexplored region: the human mind. We do not even know what mind is or how to think about its relation to the brain. Philosophers and scientists today are as divided over those questions as they have ever been. We do not yet even know for sure what consciousness is. When the brain is dead, consciousness arguably lives on. Life after death would appear to be a fully conscious life and, as though to evidence this, a small cottage industry has grown up around the retelling of out-of-body and near-death experiences. So, there is something about our capacity for thought, awareness, and memory that transcends our embodied brains.

Our knowledge, then, is amazing, but God's knowledge, like all the communicable attributes, differs from ours because it sits within God's awesome incommunicable attributes. It is one with those exalted attributes because God is not divided. In fact, all the communicable attributes have the quality of being underived, immense, immanent, timeless, and incapable of improving or deteriorating. We can't understand the communicable attributes unless we see them as being infused with these uniquely divine qualities.

So, what does the divine knowledge look like when we try to see it as possessing unfailingly those above-and-beyond-us qualities we have surveyed? Louis Berkhof's definition, so elegant it made me cry the first time I ever read it, will suffice as a starting point:

> The knowledge of God may be defined as that perfection of God whereby He, in an entirely unique manner, knows Himself and all things possible and actual in one eternal and most simple act.[1]

I remember there was something about Berkhof's ". . . in one eternal and most simple act" that left me awestruck. God isn't struggling to acquire knowledge. He needs no libraries. He is not swotting up on me late into the night, checking again the footage he has of all my past life, before he can work out how best to fix me. He is not scratching his head when I ask him to help me make the right decision. He is in possession of the facts, and already knows what will happen if I take this route or if I choose that one instead. And he accesses this knowledge in one eternal and most simple act. He can express it to us without even a moment's deliberation.

God's knowledge covers all events, thoughts, and motives, whether past, present, or future. It is absolute and unacquired. "He knows things immediately, simultaneously, exhaustively, and truly."[2]

Much of this capacity for knowing flows logically from his omnipresence. As the infinite one he was there when any given

1. Berkhof, *Systematic Theology*, 66.
2. Thiessen, *Lectures in Systematic Theology*, 81.

thing happened and is constantly present to all the things in the universe that we would ever want to know about, even down to the level of subatomic entities and laws. It goes without saying that he is also present to all that makes up the spiritual realm, so knows all about that too. And, because he is eternal, he is already present to all future events.

It is true, then, that he "knows [his] plans" (Jer 29:11). He really does know the plans he has for us. Every detail is taken care of. This is not to say, though, that foreknowledge entails fore-ordination. *Knowing* the future does not mean *fixing* the future, setting it in stone. In a complex cosmos filled with other agents that he has created: entities that might do us good, harm, or a mixture of both, it is not as though nothing and no one other than God has any say in our future. He knows every detail of this reality that we call "the future," yet, for all that, human free will is truly free. Human choices have real consequences. We do not live in a padded universe where nothing is ever going to hurt. We don't inhabit a created order in which everything has already been worked out for us without us needing to take any risks.

He loves interacting with us in the attempts we make to fulfil his destiny for us. He loves interacting with us in our often-frustrated attempts to reflect his holiness. His infinite knowledge comes into play in all of this. Yet, he has power over his powers. In order to relate to us, his attributes are always self-limited. Despite what he knows, he does not always jump in to intervene. Sometimes he does. When events leave us perplexed and hurting, we are left with the mystified but worshipful cry of Job, "Blessed be the name of the LORD" (Job 1:21). His surprises often delight us; sometimes sadden or confuse us. He is faithful like the seasons but, like the seasons, not quite predictable. A predictable god would, after all, be more of a vending machine than an object of worship.

Going back to the Berkhof quote, it's worth unpacking each point in turn. Berkhof seems to turn each glorious facet of this attribute until it catches the light, and he does this in a definite, almost poetic, order that builds progressively.

Firstly, we need to learn what we can from his knowledge *of himself*: "He, in an entirely unique manner, knows Himself. . . ." For help, let's turn to Paul in 1 Corinthians 2. Bracketed by quotations from the Old Testament about the limits of our knowledge first of the future ("Eye has not seen nor ear heard nor have entered into the heart of a man the things which God has prepared for those who love him"; 1 Cor 2:9, citing Isa 64:4), and then of present spiritual realities ("Who has known the mind of the Lord, that he will instruct him?"; 1 Cor 2:16, citing Isa 40:13), Paul tells us: "For who knows a person's thoughts except their own spirit within them? In the same way no one knows the thoughts of God except the Spirit of God" (1 Cor 2:12).

Knowing one's self might seem the least remarkable thing, and maybe that's why Berkhof starts here, and then builds up to the most remarkable thing: the unreflective, instantaneous knowing of everything. Paul, too, sees it as unremarkable that a person's thoughts would be known to themselves. What he seems to want to correct are the ideas of some who were claiming to have penetrated the heavenly realms and acquired special revelations of heavenly beings. Paul tries to remind the readers of the fact that God is a personal being, not a spiritual substance waiting to be explored in raptures of otherworldly delight. We know other humans not by studying them or contemplating them but by allowing them to disclose themselves to us. It is the same with God, says Paul. He alone possesses that knowledge of truths about himself that some were claiming to have discovered, and we cannot know them except by the indwelling Spirit of God. The Spirit reveals the deep things of God: always in a willed and personal way, not by opening our eyes to a set of abstract spiritual laws. Some were even claiming to have been given secret names of deities which could act as passwords that could usher them into the upper realms.

Granted, then, that no one can know God except as he is pleased to reveal himself to us, why is it important to note so basic a fact as the fact that God knows himself? For both Berkhof and Paul, there seems to be something special about this self-knowledge. It is somewhat more than just a rhetorical device for arguing from the least remarkable to the most remarkable. In Greek philosophy, one of the oldest aphorisms was "know yourself." How well do you know yourself? You have probably heard it said that the unreflected life is not worth living, yet, so too is the over-reflected life. Too much analysis can bring paralysis. Too much navel-gazing and we completely lose sight of the mission of God. I remain amazed by how little I have learned about myself by reflecting on my own behavior. I can rely, though, on the little flashes of insight about myself that come from *him*. When I make a mistake, instead of abandoning me in my folly, he draws even closer than before and whispers in my ear something I had not seen before. God, who knows himself, is our unfailing source of self-knowledge.

Next, Berkhof tells us that God knows "all things possible and actual." As you approach God for aid in making a big decision, remember whom you are approaching: the one who knows a word that is on your tongue before you have spoken it, the one who wrote in a book all the days appointed for you before one of them came to be (Ps 139:4, 16). He knows the truth about what *could* happen as well as what *will* happen, and the truth about everything that *has* happened. He weighs the deeds that people have already committed (1 Sam 2:3).

God knows "in one eternal and most simple act." In one vast and instantly attained knowledge of the whole universe, he knows. In one great bound of undeliberated intellectual achievement, he knows.

"He determines the number of the stars; he gives to all of them their names" (Ps 147:4). And, far beneath the stars, his understanding extends to all deeds done in the dark by people who convince themselves he will not see: "Ha! You who hide a plan too deep for the Lord, whose deeds are in the dark, and who say, 'Who sees us? Who knows us?'" (Isa 29:15). His understanding is unsearchable (Isa 40:28).

So, do you know him? He knows you. There he is, the omnipresent surveillance, resplendent within a perpetually bright and vivid awareness of all events, events that to us are either long past or part of any number of possible futures.

7

Wisdom

GOD'S WISDOM IS HIS ability to choose the highest ends and the best means possible for the attainment of those ends. Writers tend to agree on this. God's wisdom is . . .

> . . . the ability to devise perfect ends and to achieve those ends by the most perfect means.[1]

> . . . the power to see, and the inclination to choose, the best and highest goal, together with the surest means of attaining it.[2]

It means that, although our comfort is important to God, it is not the highest goal; it is not the absolute top priority. If God were the CEO of a corporation, he would devise the most perfect Gantt charts, the most impeccable workflows. He would instantly be able to balance urgency with importance, though probably what we would select as urgent he would be remarkably cool about, and what we would want to "kick into the long grass," he would make us all work on right away. God knows all possible futures so is not guessing when he selects certain things to be awarded priority.

The wisdom of God is one of the strongest ways of defending him in a world that continually questions his priorities and actions. Arguments against believing in God that fall within the "why

1. Tozer, *Knowledge of the Holy*, 66.
2. Packer, *Knowing God*, 80.

suffering?" type tend to rely on playing just two of God's attributes against each other. These two qualities are his absolute power and his total goodness or limitless love. If God is love, it is argued, he would *want* to end suffering and evil; and if God is all-powerful, he is *able* to end all suffering and evil. Yet he does not end suffering, therefore he is either not all-powerful or not very kind (or both), and hence is not worthy of our faith.

Of course, power and love are not all there is to God. We are more than twelve thousand words into this study and have, as yet, barely even mentioned either of these two attributes. What needs to happen as we respond to the "why suffering and evil?" question is that we cast our net much wider than power and love in order to get a more balanced view. And chief of these balancing attributes is wisdom. For example, in his wisdom, God seems to want humans to develop certain qualities in themselves, such as courage and compassion, and it has often enough been said that in a world without threats or hardships we would never have an opportunity to develop courage or compassion. Sometimes, God's discipline might involve people being visited with some form of evil, and God's justice might lead to the visiting of further evils upon the perpetrators of evil. So, there are times when one evil leads to a further evil for justice to be done.

God, in his wisdom, has a plan for the final defeat of evil. Jesus calls it the "kingdom of God." Jesus came announcing the reassertion of God's reign in the earth, but think for a moment about the kinds of parables he used for explaining this kingdom concept. Jesus used images of seeds sown on a variety of soils, most of which either fail to germinate or fail to produce a crop. This is a parable that tells us how much God respects the human heart. The main seat of evil is the human heart (described by Jesus as often hard, stony, or full of weeds) and for God to eradicate evil right away would be for him to eradicate you and me. The wisdom of God, however, entails the non-use of force. The wisdom of God is seen in the self-limited use of his absolute power.

It is fitting, too, that Jesus uses nature in his parables to describe the wisdom of God. Even at the height of the Enlightenment, the aging Immanuel Kant, after all his work showing the limits of what humans can know and the doubtfulness he attached to all forms of religious understanding, seemed to notice something about nature. In his *Dialectic of Teleological Judgment* no. 76–77, Kant seems to have come to question the idea that the phenomenal universe is purely mechanistic and without purpose. He finds it not only distasteful but logically highly unlikely, given the immense fine-tuning that we see all around us. He began to see a universe made up of parts that exist for the sake of wholes, a universe that is "intelligently designed."[3]

The beauty of the divine wisdom can be seen in the whole of nature, of which we are a part. It is a system in which every part exists for the sake of the whole. The finest of all the fine-tuning is perhaps most clearly seen in the way some creatures mate. We have all seen the jaw-dropping performances of male birds of paradise on the TV. Less often broadcast would be the mating game of newts. It is the more remarkable because newts are not known for their great intelligence. The male newt, when he is living in his land-lubber phase, hides under logs for most of the late summer and fall. Throughout that time, he is quite sluggish and drab looking. Come the winter, he finds somewhere frost-free to go into hibernation. Then, all of a sudden, in March, you see him in his pond. Now, he is agile and quick as a fish and, if you can catch him and look at him in a water-filled jar, you will see he has become magnificent. He is brightly colored, spotty and crested. Put him back in the pond and you will see he has become girl-crazy. Every time he finds a female, he folds his lovely crested tail in half and starts to quiver it. This wafts pheromones through the water to the female's nostrils, who usually seems entirely uninterested. However, if the male thinks he is in with a chance, he lays a tiny sperm packet on the floor of the pond. The female, who is already fat with eggs, then sits on this and somehow sucks it up through her back end. This little packet then bursts inside her and fertilizes all her eggs. All this drama is going on in our back gardens while the weather, for us, is still a bit too chilly to venture out much.

3. Critchley and Schroeder, eds., *Blackwell Companion to Continental Philosophy*, 37–39.

> The LORD by wisdom founded the earth;
>   by understanding he established the heavens;
>   by his knowledge the deeps broke forth,
>   and the clouds drop down the dew. (Prov 3:19)

Wisdom is also to be seen in man-made things, of course. I have a vivarium at home, which houses a community of tropical plants and animals. It is fascinating to watch, but it has a complex life-support system rigged up to it. There is a thermostatically-controlled adhesive heat mat stuck to the side, a water pump that creates a little creek that runs down a hollow log, a humidifier that sprays mist for twenty seconds once every six hours, day and night, and there are four lamps, two that imitate rainforest daylight for the plants, and two that give off UVB rays so that Jeffrey the gecko can create enough vitamin D3 to stay healthy. What amazes me is that each of these devices is made by a different company, yet they all work together. The vivarium manufacturer has created a bank of eight holes at the back of the lid, which are the perfect size for any tubing or mains lead that would need to be fed through, yet there is a tiny, moveable cover strip that can block the holes not in use to prevent any little critters escaping. Everything fits together perfectly to create a whole that beautifies and lights up the corner of our lounge. It has been made by wisdom.

When preachers want to encourage us to have faith in God, what they often refer to as the supreme object of that faith is his power. "Nothing is too hard for God!" they declare. Quite right. When we come to the subject of his omnipotence we will visit the many places in Scripture that tell us that nothing is impossible for him. I wonder, though, if a more resilient and contented Christian faith could be nurtured in people by holding up God's *wisdom* as the main thing about God that we must have faith in.

The main challenge here would be that we so often cannot see it. Tozer explains how God often works in the dark. In his wisdom he made the teaming wonders of the planet when darkness was on the face of the deep, he incarnated himself in the darkness of Mary's womb, died for us during some apparent eclipse of the sun, and rose again so early in the morning no one got to actually see it happen.[4] Faith in the wisdom of his workings is faith of the highest kind because it is faith in the unseen; faith in the unknown; faith in the *Deus Absconditus*. It is trust in the hidden God.

Faithfulness in the fog sooner or later is rewarded by the brilliant sunshine of God's plans becoming plain to see. Then it is that we realize, "The counsel of the LORD stands forever, the thoughts of his heart to all generations" (Ps 33:11). Then we understand that, "all things work together for good for those who love God, who are called according to his purpose" (Rom 8:28).

REFLECTION

Are you in the fog or the full light of day? Know that, whether God's counsel is clear or opaque, whether his plan is obvious (a rare thing for any of us!) or his plan is a mystery, it makes no difference. He knows the plan and the plan hasn't ever needed to change. "The counsel of the Lord stands forever."

> Deep in unfathomable mines
> Of never failing skill
> He treasures up his bright designs,
> And works his sovereign will.[5]

---

4. Tozer, *Knowledge of the Holy*, 87.
5. William Cowper, "God Moves in a Mysterious Way" (1774).

8

Integrity

God has perfect integrity. In theology, this is described as God's veracity. This word means "truthfulness" or "reliability." In ascribing veracity to God, we basically mean three things.

Firstly, *God is authentic.* He lives truthfully. What you see is what you get. He never displays any hypocrisy. He is so honest and truthful that, in Jesus of Nazareth, he counted the Pharisaic hypocrites among his very worst enemies. They were the people he denounced the most virulently (Matt 23) and set his face against most consistently. Why? Because God is the real deal, the one *true* God, the one who fully measures up to all that we would expect God to be, and he does not tolerate the opposite: those who, like whitewashed tombs, preen their outward appeal but inwardly are full of "dead men's bones and all manner of unclean things" (Matt 23:27).

The fact that the Hebrew word "amen" (fixed, sure, certain, reliable) has passed into the English language is testament to how important this attribute is. We say at the end of a prayer, "surely, certainly, verily, let it be so," because, in the very act of saying a prayer, we are exercising faith in the fact that God is certainly and reliably God.

Flowing from God's reliable nature is his faithfulness: a treasured quality both in Scripture and in the whole history of devotion to the one true God. He is always faithful: 2 Timothy 2:13: "If we are faithless, he remains faithful—for he cannot deny himself." Deuteronomy 7:9: "Know therefore that the LORD your God is God, the faithful God who maintains covenant loyalty with those who love him and keep his commandments, to a thousand generations."

Just like his wisdom, God's faithfulness is to be seen in the created order, as the hymn-writer Thomas Chisholm rightly saw:

> Summer and winter, springtime and harvest
> Sun, moon, and stars in their courses above
> Join with all nature in manifold witness
> To thy great faithfulness, mercy, and love.[1]

Creation is portrayed in Scripture as rhythmical and reliable. Night and day, and the coming of springtime, summer, fall, and winter can all be counted on. And the God who created his world that way then turns out to be the same God whose faithfulness and promises are at the heart of the message of the prophets. In the prophets, the favorite word for "faithfulness" is *hesed*, loving-kindness, covenant faithfulness: "Though the mountains be shaken, and the hills be removed, yet my unfailing love [*hesed*] for you will not be shaken" (Isa 54:10). He cannot be other than the loving and involved God that he is. Such would be to break his own veracity. His love is zealous, unconditional, and steadfast. Like the rhythms of creation, it can be relied upon. We will meet *hesed* again later on in this study.

Secondly, *God tells the truth*. There are not many things that God cannot do, but he *cannot* lie (Titus 1:2; Heb 6:18). He does not reveal everything but neither does God carefully conceal or sugar-coat the full truth. His truthful communication springs from his completely genuine character. He has nothing to hide. He is not *living* a lie, therefore he has no reason to *tell* a lie.

Positively, God's veracity means that what he says is absolutely reliable: "Has he said, and will he not do it? Or has he spoken, and will he not make it good? Behold, I have received a command to bless; he has blessed and I cannot reverse it" (Num 23:19b–20). What he has promised will surely come to pass: "For in him every

---

1. From the hymn of 1923, "Great Is Thy Faithfulness."

one of God's promises is a 'Yes.' For this reason it is through him that we say the 'Amen,' to the glory of God" (2 Cor 1:20).

Thirdly, *God has created us in his truthful image.* We are made by a real and truthful God so are gifted with the capacity to see things the way they really are. The famous French philosopher René Descartes, while he sat next to a stove trying to figure out what there was out of all the things he knew that could not be doubted, feared that his whole grasp upon reality might be an elaborate hoax inspired by a mischievous demon.[2] But then he concluded that God would not have made us with minds that are continuously in error. Capable of error we surely are, but our minds were shaped for the truth and we still have an instinct for the truth. We have a nose for it. This is why we have judges and juries. We think that, under normal circumstances, they will deliberate without fear or favor, based on the evidence, and pronounce a safe sentence. And this despite the fact that everyone involved in a case will be deeply flawed, guilty of their own misdemeanors and vices, and host to an assortment of prejudices and biases.

REFLECTION

God is the real deal, he speaks the truth and he imparts to us an instinct for the truth. In every way, he lines up with himself. All the way down he is what he is. God, would you give us the power be true followers of Christ even when no one's looking? Amen.

2. Descartes, *Meditations*, 106.

9

Holiness

Holiness is an extremely important attribute of God. It should be understood as absolutely suffusing all his other attributes. The holiness of God was so prominent in Israelite thinking that "Holy One" became one of their favorite terms of address for him (Isa 5:19; 30:12; 43:3; 55:5).

That God is holy means two things. First and foremost, it means that God is *separate*. The Hebrew word for holy is *qadesh*, which is from *qad* meaning to cut or separate. It means that God is wholly other, a descriptor we already used in chapter 4 when we looked at the singular uniqueness of God. The fact that we have come back to the same terminology is evidence that discreet categorizations of God are impossible and folly to even attempt. What we do have are angles. From this angle we view God's otherness as the source of our fear of God. This majestic holiness of God is a source of the sanest kind of terror. If we have not grasped that there is something ultimately terrifying about God, then we have never truly approached him but have approached instead some idol of the mind.

Rudolf Otto's work on this has been constantly referred to and quoted ever since his book *Das Heilige* (The Holy) came out in 1917. Its English translation, *Idea of the Holy*, appeared in 1923. He set himself the task of trying to define, and to encourage experiences of, that nonrational, uncanny feeling we get when we detect that we are in the presence of a vastly greater being. He tried creating long periods of silence in the liturgies he wrote in the hope of encouraging experiences of awe among the worshippers. A few extracts from his book will help us as he unpacks for us what he calls the "numinous," the creature-feeling we get when we are in the presence of the overpowering *otherness* of God. Encountering the holiness of God brings "the hushed, trembling, and speechless humility of the creature in the presence of—whom or what? In the presence of that which is a Mystery inexpressible and above all creatures."[1] He speaks of a holy shudder: "Here we have a terror fraught with an inward shuddering such as not even the most menacing and overpowering created thing can instil."[2] To be before God is to experience "a consciousness of the absolute superiority and supremacy of a power other than myself."[3] God's holiness produces in us the feeling that "man, in his 'profaneness,' is not worthy to stand in the presence of the Holy One, and that his entire personal unworthiness might even defile holiness itself."[4]

This lofty, numinous aspect of God's holiness is sometimes captured in the arts. When I taught on a course called Creative Arts, Mission, and Ministry, I would often discuss with the students what that certain something-or-other might be that separates a great piece of art from something that is merely good. Otto's "numinous" was the best word I could find for it. Yet, how to create it eluded us in our classroom discussions. That quality is made even more elusive by the fact that it is often to be encountered in works produced by creators who care little about faith. Mark Rothko's enormous planes of shimmering color, for example, are overwhelming to behold. The same is true of many classical pieces of music. Though I could easily choose Handel or Bach at this point, it is Richard Strauss that takes the prize, in my view, for having produced the piece of music with the loftiest numinous quality. The one I am thinking of is *Also Sprach Zarathustra* Op.30 Prelude,

1. Otto, *Idea of the Holy*, 13.
2. Otto, *Idea of the Holy*, 14.
3. Otto, *Idea of the Holy*, 22.
4. Otto, *Idea of the Holy*, 56.

also known as *Sunrise,* the theme popularized by *2001: A Space Odyssey.* It is little more than a minute long yet speaks remarkably clearly of God's mystery and wonder combined with the rush of exalted and hopeful feelings that meeting God often produces in us. Yet, for all that, it was inspired by the overtly anti-Christian ideas of Strauss's friend Friedrich Nietzsche. More recently, U2's "Bullet the Blue Sky," from the 1987 album *The Joshua Tree,* would be an example of numinous music written from a faith perspective. It is about as punchy and dirty as rock can get before it tips over into a wall of noise. And, although originating purely as an instrumental jam, the lyrics that were added are full of political rage against American military intervention in El Salvador and Nicaragua during the Regan administration. Beyond this, it defies description, which is always the mark, I believe, of success for any form of nonliterary creation. So, these are the kinds of portals that grant us glimpses, accommodated to us, of what Otto meant by the numinous aspect of the holiness of God. But there is another aspect.

The other aspect of God's holiness is his *ethical purity.* He is separated from evil and sin (Job 34:10; Ps 92:15; Hab 1:13). "God is light and in him there is no darkness at all" (1 John 1:5). He is purer than the look in an infant's eyes, more spotless than untrodden snow, more sacred than lovers, more perfect than a cloudless sky, more virtuous than the timely help of a stranger, more righteous than Luther King's most stirring speech, and more saintly than a kind old lady with your children. His holiness is lovely and loving, gracious in its purity, transforming in its power.

The English countryside has always held a fascination for me because it is the product of centuries of negotiation between nature and humans. It has wildness but each patch of wildness is neatly bounded. We have few large forests, but lots and lots of little woodlands: little dark green woolly patches on a hillside, each one contained within a fascinatingly irregular "rectangle," the very shape of the boundary being the product of ancient property rights or the winding path of a creek. Then there are the hedges: some have been allowed to grow into strips of woodland, others are closely shorn but dotted with trees that the farmer has allowed to grow. Each field is a patchwork of crops sown in beautiful lines that follow the irregular shapes of the hedges. Some of the fields are meadows grazed by cattle or sheep. In the meadows there is the occasional large tree in the middle where livestock can find shade. Little dwellings and narrow lanes only enhance the landscape, they seldom scar it: in many cases a vista would not be the same *without* that perfectly positioned farmhouse nestling between the trees. Such scenes have been idealized often enough, of course, on boxes of fudge or cookies, and on many a postcard and painting, and the poets of England have long reserved their best lines for its gentle landscapes. It is a world of symbiotic negotiations, of beautifully contained wildnesses.

The picture I've painted here is my way of approaching the subject of our own personal holiness. Just like the bounded wildness of the Devonshire of my childhood, God harnesses and contains our capacities. Many of our unholy behaviors are unbounded good behaviors. They are driven by desires for things that are essentially good, such as power or intimacy, but which have gone horribly wrong. Similarly, Aristotle reckoned that most human vices are just extreme versions of virtues. In fact, he thought there are often two opposite extremes, with true virtue lying somewhere in the middle, which he called the Golden Mean. Cowardice and folly, for example, are opposite poles of behavior, with courage lying exactly in the middle: audacious but not stupid. With God there is much more than mere moderation involved, of course. When we see God we see the everlasting, ever-consistent standard, the straight edge that shows up our extremes, the light that shows us just how dark our unbridled passions and appetites have become. But with regular cultivation, virtue fructifies just as verdantly as in Devon's fields of barley.

The following classic passage, with which we will finish, expresses both senses of God's holiness: his majestic *transcendence* and his spotless *moral purity*:

> In the year that King Uzziah died, I saw the LORD sitting
> on a throne, high and lofty; and the hem of his robe filled
> the temple. Seraphs were in attendance above him; each
> had six wings: with two they covered their faces, and

with two they covered their feet, and with two they flew. And one called to another and said:

> "Holy, holy, holy is the LORD of hosts;
> the whole earth is full of his glory."

The pivots on the thresholds shook at the voices of those who called, and the house filled with smoke. And I said: "Woe is me! I am lost, for I am a man of unclean lips, and I live among a people of unclean lips; yet my eyes have seen the King, the LORD of hosts!" (Isa 6:1–5)

REFLECTION

It is this attribute of God that most clarifies why there is such a thing as "atonement." This is the very next thing that the helpful seraph attending to the awe-struck Isaiah brings into the equation: "Then one of the seraphs flew to me, holding a live coal that had been taken from the altar with a pair of tongs. The seraph touched my mouth with it and said: 'Now that this has touched your lips, your guilt has departed and your sin is blotted out.'"

The same apostle that terrifies us with the assertion that "God is light and in him is no darkness at all," assures us moments later that "The blood of Jesus Christ his Son cleanses us from all sin" (1 John 1:5, 7).

Seek God now for a fresh cleansing of your spirit through the sacrifice that God has provided.

10

Justice

The justice of God and the righteousness of God are synonymous terms. Both are a quality within the divine being that means that God has an impeccable standard and expectation of what is good and right. And both entail the exercising of that quality when confronted—and confronted is the right word—with human hubris and defiance. Hence, the Bible speaks of God giving to everyone according to what they deserve: rewards for righteous behavior (Heb 6:10; Matt 25:21, 34; Rom 2:6–7), and penalties for unrighteous behavior. God shows *restorative justice* of the highest kind but, for now, it is good to note that his *retributive justice* is an inescapable reality (Rev 16:5–6; Rom 2:5–11). This retribution from God is what we mean by the wrath of God, his holy revulsion at that which is the contradiction of his holiness. It is both a wrath "to come" (1 Thess 1:10) and it is a wrath emanating from God now (Rom 1:18). Again, terrifying!

Yet, there is a very unexpected twist with this one. Nowhere is this brought out more clearly than in the first three chapters of Paul's letter to the Romans. The argument Paul uses is in the style of what is known as a "prophetic lawsuit."[1] The case against humanity in Romans 1–3 builds and builds until it becomes obvious that no one—neither the openly debauched nor those that might appear more upright; and neither gentiles nor Jews—can expect to

1. Prothro, *Both Judge and Justifier*, 3–4.

get away with anything. Paul concludes: "Now we know that whatever the law says, it speaks to those who are under the law, so that every mouth may be silenced, and the whole world may be held accountable to God" (Rom 3:19). But then there is the surprise verdict: "But now, apart from law, the righteousness of God has been disclosed"(Rom 3:21). Here, Paul uses the term "righteousness" *not* to describe God's just judgment and wrath but to describe the way he *saves* us, with the result that we can all be "justified by his grace as a gift" (Rom 3:24). Just when we were expecting a verdict of condemnation, there is a verdict of justification. The same righteousness that condemns can also justify. Thus, an attribute of God that announces our failure to meet expectations, has become the very attribute that gets us acquitted at the judgment bar.

Of all the attributes of God, it is the righteousness and justice of God that places us in the most peril. Even the matchless holiness of God is not necessarily a danger to us, for it is in his righteousness that God *expresses* his holiness when he encounters sin. And it is this *expression* of unsettled holiness in the face of human rebellion that barred the way to fellowship. But now that very righteousness that would have been our undoing, instead of being unleashed on us, has been conferred on us. Instead of falling upon us like an avalanche, it clothes us like a fine robe. Instead of being the thing we dreaded more than death itself, it is now the very thing that is right at the heart of salvation. Condemnation was the heart of the problem; justification by faith in Christ is the heart of the answer.

What can we compare this to? It is like that moment when you are called before the boss, or the head teacher, or the principal. You are not told what the meeting will be about and, of course, you believe the worst. You are going to be fired, you are going to be suspended, expelled, punished. Why? Because you don't just *think* you deserve it; you *know* you deserve it! Then, the unexpected happens. All the solemnity you were expecting is there. The face has the same grave expression it always has as you are offered a seat. But, just a few sentences in and you are pinching yourself. You cannot believe it. Not only have you entirely got away with whatever wrongs you know you have done, you are now being offered a promotion, an opportunity, an award. You are getting the opposite of what you know should be coming your way.

God specializes in these moments. These surprise moments are what he loves to bring about. Spiritually, you know that you have not been at your best all week, then someone asks you to preach. You have made a mess of things, then someone asks you to take on a position in the pastoral team.

The other side to what he does—the actual visitation of judgment—is described (even in the Old Testament; that part of the Bible people most associate with judgment and wrath, even there) as his "strange work" (Isa 28:21). He takes no delight in it (Ezek 18:23), yet, when it comes to some of the evil rulers and regimes in our world, we are profoundly grateful when it does happen. If his justice had not brought down apartheid, or the Berlin Wall, where would we be today? God is just. He exercises retributive justice upon evil when he absolutely has to, knowing that, whatever he visits upon one person will likely bring suffering upon many others too. But what he prefers is that we already come to realize we are without excuse before the face of the Lord. Then, he likes to surprise us with a tsunami of mercy.

REFLECTION

You are now righteous with the very righteousness of God. Faith has joined you to Christ and now all that is his has become yours. It means you can breathe. It means you do not have to fear human expectations. All divine expectations are met, so what does it matter what people think of you, or your performance or looks or merits or faults? God the judge of all, before whom we will all one day stand, has conferred his very own righteousness upon you.

11

Love

This is the point at which there is the possibility of paradox and even contradiction. There is the possibility that the love of God *negates* the justice of God. This could happen in two senses. The love of God, if it really is immense and free, cancels out immediately any sense in which God wants to judge or punish sin, and possibly even cancels out the need for God's righteousness to be conferred upon us: why would we need that if, thanks to God's love, we were not in any danger of judgment in the first place? But the opposite danger is the more serious since it can be a position held with the most ardent conviction; with the conviction that orthodoxy itself is being defended against a mighty onslaught. By this I mean that we can elevate God's inscrutable and unchanging justice to such an extent that God *cannot* act in love toward people, or at least cannot act in love toward people unless they have first embraced God's justification. The doctrine of justification can thus be reified to such a degree that we actually end up with the opposite of what was intended: a picture of God that is so very austere that the *only* way of being on the receiving end of anything other than a blast of heavenly wrath is to slip inside the righteousness of the Son, hidden from the only-just-contained rage of the Father.

Thankfully, we are not alone in seeing that there is a certain tension here. The biblical writers saw it too. After all, why would it even be worth marveling at that "righteousness and peace will kiss each other" (Ps 85:10b). The psalmist assumes that righteous judgment coming from heaven and a peaceful life on earth for those deserving of judgment is a contradiction. And surely it is. Or, why would Paul need to affirm that God has been both "just and the justifier of the one who has faith in Jesus" (Rom 3:26), unless there was an inevitable tension between showing justice on the one hand and justifying sinners on the other?

The Edwardian theologian P. T. Forsyth would resolve the tension using the wonderful phrase "holy love." By this he meant that God's love is only ever a *holy* love, never a doting, unprincipled outpouring of sentimentality. But, conversely, God's holiness is only ever a *loving* holiness: the very fact that it goes out from the Godhead into the realm of human sinfulness to graciously deal with sin through the cross is an act of both love and holiness, according to Forsyth. It means that, even when God is letting you know how holy he is, you are safe. He never stops being love personified when he needs to be holiness personified. You won't die. He is holy with a holy *love*.

We can also say that whenever God brings judgment, he does so in a way that earnestly desires the *good* of humanity. Love for another, according to Thomas Aquinas, is "to wish that person good."[1] We can say that God's holiness also wishes people good, even if there must first be some corrective suffering.

So, we have a loving holiness that culminates in the cross, and a loving holiness that, though bringing judgment, does so for the good of people. In both cases love and holiness move in tandem. They do not cancel each other out.

Both sides of this equation: holiness and love, share in the same sense of a *mysterium tremendum*. They are both unoriginate; both equally unprompted; both flowing from the same inexhaustible source.

It was to be many years before I would come face-to-face with God's love. It came in response to prayer. I had been asking that God would, in the words of Ephesians 3:18, make me able to "comprehend, with all the saints, what is the breadth and length

---

1. Aquinas, *Summa Theologiae*, Prima Pars, Question 20, Article 1.

and height and depth, to know the love of Christ that surpasses knowledge." About a year passed before God suddenly answered. There came a series of sudden jolts when I went about my business. I could be anywhere: walking down a street, sitting in a coffee shop, sitting in an airport lounge. I would be deluged by an awareness of how much God loved me: *me* in particular, that is. J. I. Packer rightly points out that God's love is not a "vague, diffused goodwill toward everyone in general and nobody in particular."[2] Precisely because it is so vast, precisely because it bears the stamp of God's immensity, it can be *infinitely personalized*; immanent to each person. When we are face-to-face with it, we feel as though there is no one else in the world.

Each time I encountered this personalized love I was desperately aware of how undeserving I was of such special care. I was aware of God walking with me, looking after me, smoothing my way and taking great personal interest in me. On the airport lounge occasion, I was in a Muslim country and I was sat quite close to a long prayer mat. A woman who looked terribly miserable came to the mat. She began doing all the right things that her religion expected of her. She was bowing in the right way on the mat, doing it the right number of times, and reciting all the right things under her breath. Yet, for all that, she seemed just as unhappy when she arose as when she first knelt to pray. True, the same can be said of many Christians, but that isn't the point I'm making. My point is that I felt that surely, she, of all the people in that lounge, was more deserving of this love than I was. She had truly tried. I had not. I had been sheerly gifted with it. I had been traveling alone and had been aware of God taking care of me all that morning. I even had exactly the right amount of spare currency to buy something I wanted in the duty free. Without any effort from me, God had been with me. I saw her and burst into tears. This experience was like the others in that it was more than just feeling moved. It was more like being crushed. It was a suddenly bright and clear apprehension of how unmerited, how unprompted, God's love for me was. Had the language barrier not prevented me—and were I able to recover my

2. Packer, *Knowing God*, 140.

composure before she left—I might have ventured to say something to her, but what I would have said I cannot imagine. A waiter asked if I wanted a coffee. He must have thought I'd just had some terrible news. Quite the opposite.

Over time, these revelations of God's love came to define me. Don't get me wrong, I am a massive work in progress, but to this day those encounters with God's love guide my decisions and reactions to things, probably more than I am conscious of. God's love gave me a lens that suggests to me all the time that giving and more giving, forgiving and more forgiving, will always be the best way. It changed my life.

The way God's love is so immense, so measureless, is perfectly captured by this hymn, made famous by George Beverly Shea:

> The love of God is greater far
> Than tongue or pen can ever tell.
> It goes beyond the highest star
> And reaches to the lowest hell.
>
> Could we with ink the oceans fill
> Or were the skies of parchment made
> Were every stalk on earth a quill
> Or every man a scribe by trade:
>
> To write the love of God above
> Would drain the ocean dry
> Nor could the scroll contain the whole
> Though stretched from sky to sky.[3]

Not only is God's love shot through by his infinity, it also bears the stamp of God's self-existence. Remember how we saw that God is the uncaused cause of everything else? God's love, nestling as it does within God's self-existence, is unoriginated. Nothing external to God has prompted it. It comes to us like an unprovoked attack— of love. He loves us because he *is* love. This is what John means when he says that God *first loved us*: "In this is love, not that we loved God but that he loved us and sent his Son to be the atoning sacrifice for our sins" (1 John 4:10).

3. Frederick Lehman, "The Love of God" (1917).

Many years after those sudden jolts I described, I had a further encounter with God's love. By now I was married with three children and happily working as a theology lecturer at Cliff College. I was taking a rest in an empty office next to my own and sitting in a window seat that looked out of a large bay window within the very oldest part of the oldest building on the campus: the part that was once an eighteenth-century country house, bought by a part of the famous Guinness dynasty, Henry Gratton-Guinness, and then donated by him to become a missionary training home. I prayed, and, as I prayed, I became acutely aware that God had, in fact, *always* loved me. There was never a time when he did not. Long before I ever even acknowledged him, and all through the times when I lived in open defiance of him, and all through the times when my life as a Christian had not been what it ought to be, he loved me. In fact, I was aware of how there was something deep inside me that was disappointed that God had not been more affected by my sin. Not only were all the good things I had done *not* in the equation, but all the things I had done *against* him had not made even the slightest dent. I was disappointed that he was not hurt by me. He loved me just the same, and because he always had, I was assured that he always would. This reminds me of a quote from Spurgeon I often give to my students: "When we had not as yet one throb of spiritual feeling, one pulse of hope, or one breath of desire, the Lord loved us even then!"[4] And, of course, this is what the New Testament confirms: "But God proves his love for us in that while we still were sinners Christ died for us" (Rom 5:8).

We may not have fully resolved the tension we started with in this chapter. But we have, hopefully, safeguarded both God's righteousness *and* his love. We have glimpsed a little of how they do not obliterate one another, yet neither do they stand in schizophrenic opposition to each other. Rather, they move in tandem together: his love moving him to make a way for his righteousness to became a saving thing for us. Because of that, we can all move closer to him, basking in that intimacy with him for which we were created. And we saw that both God's holiness and his love share in the same

---

4. Spurgeon, "Love's Birth and Parentage," in *Spurgeon's Sermons*, vol. 22.

awesome, unoriginate majesty that is native to this self-existent, immense God.

REFLECTION

God wants you to know that he loves you. Try praying with Paul (Eph 3:14–19), that you would be able to comprehend the full extent of God's love. Keep on asking for this personal revelation of his love, and you *will* receive.

12

Goodness

WE CAN REFER TO God's goodness in a very general sense to describe his moral perfection but here we mean specifically his kindness and bounty toward all that he has made. This goodness can be seen, first, in the *delight* he takes in all that he has made: "God saw everything that he had made, and indeed, it was very good" (Gen 1:31).

God would appear, secondly, to be moved by this delight to be good and kind toward all that he has made: "The LORD is good to all, and his compassion is over all that he has made. . . . The eyes of all look to you, and you give them their food in due season. You open your hand, satisfying the desire of every living thing" (Ps 145:9, 15–16).

Thirdly, we can also say that God's good creation is itself an *expression* of his bounty and goodwill toward us:

> You visit the earth and water it,
>   you greatly enrich it;
> the river of God is full of water;
>   you provide the people with grain,
>   for so you have prepared it.
> You water its furrows abundantly,
>   settling its ridges,
> softening it with showers,
>   and blessing its growth.
> You crown the year with your bounty;
>   your wagon tracks overflow with richness. (Ps 65:9–11)

This is an important aspect of what God does to inspire faith. It is this goodness of God that leads us to repentance (Rom 2:4). God, "has not left himself without a witness," says Paul while preaching to the people of Iconium, "in doing good—giving you rains from heaven and fruitful seasons, and filling you with food and your hearts with joy" (Acts 14:17).

All three of these aspects of God's goodness are of topical significance. Firstly, we need to share in God's delight in his creation. People seem to greet the move toward greener lifestyles as a burdensome obligation, a kind of "party's over" moment. We are having to sober up to the realities of what we have done to the planet. Yet, if we would all make delighting in nature into a regular feature of our lives, being kind to the environment would not seem burdensome. British naturalist Chris Packham even goes so far as to claim that many of us today suffer from "biophobia," or "nature phobia." We have grown so alienated from nature that we see it purely as an enemy to be tamed, contained, or destroyed. He laments that children and young people are even losing some of the nature vocabulary that was once commonplace: words like "conker" and "newt" having been replaced by "chatroom" and "database" in one recent new edition of a children's dictionary.[1] We seem to be losing our connections with the natural world, making it more of an effort to care for than it should be. It is a miracle that environmental activism is strongest among the young: those typically least connected to nature.

By the time I was sixteen, after a typically 1970's childhood of playing outside all the time, pond-dipping, and tree-climbing, my family moved to a lovely house at the western end of the Cotswold Hills in the West Country of England. The soft limestone had been deeply cut by the veins of little rivers on their way to the River Severn, the river dividing most of England from most of Wales. The result of these deep cuts in the limestone was that virtually every tree and every meadow was on a steep incline. Even the spaces between, up on the plateaus between the wooded valleys, were not farmed very intensively. Such amazing expanses as the undulating

---

1. Packham and McCubbin, *Back to Nature*, 16–17.

and wildflower-rich Minchinhampton Common, just visible from my bedroom window, and its adjoining Rodborough Common have been the inspiration for writers. One of the valleys was the location for the novel *Cider with Rosie*. The royal family seemed to like the county. Prince Charles lived in Badminton in the east, but others preferred this westerly end of the Cotswolds. Princess Michael of Kent lived across the valley from us, and Princess Anne was just up another valley, in fact, I think she owned most of it.

The only way I could cope with the beauty all around me was to name it, bring it under the power of a word. Before long, I could name every species of wildflower I encountered on any walk. Most of these flowers were deliciously diminutive. They were understated and pretty, eking out a happy existence on some steep and closely grazed horse paddock that had never seen a modern plough nor felt the spray of weed killer. I knew where the bee orchids were. I knew where the wild box grew. Our valley was called Toadsmoor Valley, and it certainly had plenty of toads. The valley was accessed from our village via the most ridiculously steep lane. This lane ran past the village church, which sat precariously on the edge of the valley beside a sheer drop. The opposite flank of the valley was sumptuously clothed in pure, uninterrupted beechwood. At the bottom of the valley was a fishing lake. The scene was a tourist attraction waiting to be discovered, a moist wooded paradise filled all the way up to Lypiatt Park, where Guy Faulks's gunpowder plot was plotted, with innumerable natural wonders. Each autumn set the whole countryside ablaze with the deep coppers and golds of the innumerable beech trees. I was learning my trees at the time and the beech became my firm favorite, with its majestic smooth trunk, handsome crown, and glossy leaves that, whether in their spring freshness or autumn rusts, always looked good—in contrast to the sudden wilting and dumping of the ash, which then has the temerity to be the last of the forest trees to come back into leaf in the spring.

It is not an effort to drive an electric car, have a renewable energy contract, pick up someone else's litter or someone else's dog poop. It is not an effort to create wildlife habitats in the garden and spend time reading packaging to see whether it can go in the recycling or not. It is a delight, because God's creation is so delight-ful. It is still a beautiful world we live in.

Secondly, God is good toward his creation. Even with seven billion lovely people gracing our earth, there ought be enough to feed us all. There is no lack in God's generous supply, but nature's bounty is constantly short-circuited by human greed, leading to declines in fertility and a grossly uneven distribution of produce. If we had more respect for God, we would not be worshipping wealth and profit. If we had more respect for God, we would have more respect for the land and for one another.

Thirdly, the environment is not only important for the reasons that are obvious, but it is important to us as Christians because it is part of God's mission. The goodness of God displayed by nature's bounty is an important witness to the divine nature. In fact, it's so important that Paul thinks that to ignore the witness that nature bears to its creator is to render oneself "without excuse" (Rom 1:20). We can help in allowing nature to bear its unique form of witness, hence the fifth of the five marks of mission of the Anglican Communion, added in 1990, is "to strive to safeguard the integrity of creation, and sustain and renew the life of the earth."[2]

REFLECTION

1. What will you do to ensure that connecting with nature and delighting in it is a regular part of your life?
2. Is there anything you can do, as a consumer, to limit the impact of greed upon the abundance of nature? Are there more sustainable ways to shop for clothes and food; or is there a more sustainable diet you could follow?
3. What might you do directly to enhance the little piece of nature that you might have direct control over?

2. "Marks of Mission," Anglican Communion, https://www.anglicancommunion.org/mission/marks-of-mission.aspx.

13

Grace

God's grace is specifically his love and favor as it is experienced when it comes into contact with the ill-deserving. I have already said much about that, but I would add the following three points.

Let grace be grace. Some of the theologians I have read while preparing this book seem to turn God's grace into its opposite. They so emphasize our ill-desert and so focus on the human pride that prevents us from being able to humbly receive grace that they effectively cancel grace. To them, God's grace is seemingly nothing other than a severe rebuke to our pride.

Another thing that often happens is that the people of God are prevented from being able to really savor this attribute. Those charged with discipling the flock of God are too eager to avoid giving the impression that one can accept salvation purely by grace and then live however you like. Paul, of course, encountered that very issue as a result of preaching grace all the time. Three times in Romans (3:8; 6:1, 15) he counters the accusations that had been flying around that he was preaching something along the lines of: "that's right, forget the law of Moses: just keep on sinning as much as you can because the more you sin the more God's grace will abound!" It's what we call the "antinomian accusation." Antinomianism means the stance that some have taken that is "anti" "nomos"—anti-law. It is the view that no moral guidance need ever be given. Under this new age of grace people can be relied on to instinctively know right from wrong and will be empowered by the Spirit to always do what is right. We see from Galatians 5:16 that Paul did indeed have immense faith in the power of the Spirit to keep his people walking in the right way and to keep them from yielding to the flesh. Yet, this did not mean that he shied away from giving moral guidance; he often quotes from the Ten Commandments.

What we can say, though, is that for Paul to be accused so often of antinomianism must mean that he was very much laying the stress on God's free grace and not jumping in immediately with a whole list of caveats. And we should be like that too. His message was open to misunderstanding. How open to misunderstanding is ours? Paul was unrelenting in his proclamation that justifying grace must be received by faith "from first to last" (Rom 1:17). The Christian life carries on just as it began: by grace through faith. If not then "grace is no longer grace" (Rom 11:6), according to Paul. Grace is truly free. It is the most sincerely free gift anyone can ever receive. And, like any free gift, it can be misunderstood.

Let grace empower you. It is surprising how often God's grace is referred to not merely as the source of our salvation (e.g., Acts 15:11; Rom 3:24; Eph 2:8–9; Titus 3:7, 11) but also as the source of our ongoing empowerment: "For sin shall no longer be your master, because you are not under the law, but under grace" (Rom 6:14); "But by the grace of God I am what I am, and his grace to me was not without effect. No, I worked harder than all of them—yet not I, but the grace of God that was with me" (1 Cor 15:10); "But he said to me, 'My grace is sufficient for you, for my power is made perfect in weakness'" (2 Cor 12:9); "You then, my son, be strong in the grace that is in Christ Jesus" (2 Tim 2:1); and these are just a small sample of passages. In the New Testament, encountering God's grace is an experience that leaves a person changed forever. It is described in a way remarkably like the way the inward empowerment of the Spirit is described. In fact, one could almost swap the phrase "grace of God" for "Spirit of God" without significantly altering the meaning. This is indeed a work of the Spirit. It is about the way God strengthens us at times when we feel that we are not entitled to it. Power seems to come from nowhere. We have, perhaps, not even asked for it. Power to perform a task well might come at a time when we feel we have not been living a particularly worthy or good life. Or, power to live a good and worthy life comes to us in a way that we cannot explain and did nothing to contribute to.

Put grace at the heart of your proclamation. The preaching of the gospel is sometimes abbreviated simply as the preaching of grace. Paul's task was "the task of testifying to the good news of God's grace" (Acts 20:24). Signs and wonders were expected to accompany the proclaiming of this message of grace. At Iconium, Paul and Barnabas remained for a long while preaching boldly, and the Lord "testified to the word of his grace by granting signs and wonders to be done through them" (Acts 14:3; cf. Heb 2:3–4). It seems that when we center our preaching around God's gracious invitation and his welcome toward the undeserving, we attract God's affirmation and confirmation. He says. "Yes! That's what I want people to hear!"

REFLECTION

I invite you take one of these three points: that grace should be allowed to be grace, that grace can empower us, and that grace should be the heart of our message, and think on it. What can you do or might you change to become a person more defined by grace?

14

Mercy

Mercy is enormously significant, especially within ancient Israel. When God meets with Moses to enlarge upon his "I AM" definition of himself, the quality he mentions first is his mercy:

> The LORD passed before him, and proclaimed, "The LORD, the LORD, a God merciful and gracious, slow to anger, and abounding in steadfast love and faithfulness."
> (Exod 34:6)

This is a great passage to start with as it uses both of the Hebrew words that are commonly translated as "mercy": *racham* and *hesed.*

Racham is the word that underlies the word "merciful" in our passage. The various forms of this word are often translated with terms such as "tender mercy" or "compassion," but also, surprisingly, the same root can mean "womb." Lexicons are not unanimous that *racham* derives in some way from an original reference to the womb, but a search of the internet will reveal that the idea is an understandably popular one. If there is a relationship to the womb then this word would carry some sense of the tender, protective and, indeed, unconditional love that a mother-to-be has for the life that is in her womb. The unborn child has not yet done anything either to earn her favor or to annoy her, so this is a completely unprompted and instinctive care and compassion. Given that God freely compares his own compassion to that of both a father (Ps 103:13: "As a father has compassion for his children, so the LORD has compassion for those who fear him") and a mother (Isa 49:15: "Can a woman forget her nursing child, or show no compassion for the child of her womb?"), this way of interpreting *racham* does not seem too wide of the mark even if derivation from "womb" cannot be proven.

Hesed, the word translated as "steadfast love" in the passage above, is a term we have already met. This word, even more than *racham*, has generated a small cottage industry of webpages, vlogs, and books discussing its significance. Whole conferences take place unpacking the full meaning of *hesed*. It is often held to be untranslatable, and while that claim is probably a little overstated, the significance of the term, both to ancient Israel and to modern Judaism, is rightly celebrated. Its true heir within the New Testament is probably not so much the straightforward *eleos*, mercy, but the profound Christian concept of *agape* (love): a word definitive of the early Christian community and a catch-all term for describing what God had done in Christ for undeserving humanity, especially favored in John's Gospel and letters (e.g., 1 John 4:7–11). *Hesed* has taken on a similarly definitive significance within Judaism. Rabbi Simlai summed up this sentiment in the Talmud by saying: "Torah begins with an act of benevolence [*hesed*] and ends with an act of benevolence [*hesed*]."[1] He means that Torah begins with God's kind act of making coats of skin for Adam and Eve after they had sinned, and concludes with the death of Moses and the loving care with which God buries him.

The root of *hesed* is about ardent desire or zeal. This ardent desire can be a negative thing: a strong antipathy toward someone, but most often it signifies the zealous devotion of a worshipper toward God, or the undying love of God toward his people. Where *racham* leaves us in no doubt that this mercy is unprompted, *hesed* leaves us in no doubt as to its sincerity. It is not mere tolerance. It is not cool. It is a *red hot* kind of love. God's love is pure initiative. Yet, Paul tells us that love is both "patient" and "kind" (1 Cor 13:4). It is both reactive and proactive. When we see it at work, love is usually bearing stuff. Its routine *modus operandi* is to tolerate the lack of

---

1. Sotah 14a:6.

love in others and resist temptations into those unloving behaviors. It is in reactive mode. But what love loves to do is take the initiative, to be proactive. It loves to not merely tolerate others but to donate itself to others. It likes to say or do something completely out-of-the-blue. This is when love gets to be red hot, after days of biding its time. Love finally gets to be itself.

His mercy is new every morning: "The steadfast love [from *hesed*] of the LORD never ceases, his mercies [from *racham*] never come to an end; they are new every morning; great is your faithfulness" (Lam 3:22–23). God is eternally self-renewing so this should not surprise us. His mercy never flags. He never, ever gets compassion fatigue. His mercy lasts forever: "O give thanks to the LORD, for he is good, for his steadfast love [from *hesed*] endures forever" (Ps 136:1).

God's mercy is extended to the unappreciative, and we must do likewise: ". . . for he is kind to the ungrateful and the wicked. Be merciful, just as your Father is merciful" (Luke 6:36). Here, the Greek word for "merciful" is *oiktirmōn*. It signifies an attitude of deep empathy and pity, in this case, toward those who are doing nothing obvious to arouse such feelings. It's classical Greek origin, *oitktos*, can signify weeping and wailing with pity or grief.[2]

Mercy motivated the ministry of Jesus: "As he went ashore, he saw a great crowd; and he had compassion for them, because they were like sheep without a shepherd; and he began to teach them many things" (Mark 6:34), and here: "When he went ashore, he saw a great crowd; and he had compassion for them and cured their sick" (Matt 14:14). In both of these passages, the Greek word for "compassion" is from the noun *splanchna*, meaning "bowels." There is a form of this word that would literally mean "many bowelled," and is the word used to describe God's attitude to toward Job in James 5:11. Our equivalent anatomical metaphor would be to use the heart. We would say, "big hearted" instead of "many bowelled," or, in the passage above, we would say that Christ's *heart* was moved for the people. But my point is that both Greek words (*oiktirmos* and *splanchna*) are used to describe a feeling that is deep

---

2. Liddel and Scott, *Greek-English Lexicon*, 479.

enough to result in *action*. They are visceral, bodily terms. The body *does* something in response to such feelings: we can hardly help ourselves.

So, we have surveyed terms that describe a nurturing but un-prompted care and protection toward the helpless, a passionate and initiative-seizing desire for the good of another, and a state of being deeply moved, to one's very bowels, by a need. In every case, those whom God feels so much empathy for are not doing anything to warrant this or deserve it.

Likewise, when we are invited to join in with God's pity we are not expected to wait for the objects of our mercy to become likeable, or even grateful. It is, I suppose, a little like my relationship with animals. Most people have no difficulty in liking fluffy creatures: animals with big sad eyes, cute faces, and strokeable fur. Whereas I like the creatures that crawl around at night or hang out in waterlogged places, many of which get a very bad press in fairy tales. I mean: toads, newts, salamanders, frogs, lizards. I even rather like insects and spiders.

REFLECTION

Ask God to stir your heart for the toads of our world, not just the kittens. I mean that metaphorically, of course. Perhaps make a start by praying for one that you know well.

15

Longsuffering

ONE BIBLE TEACHER I used to love listening to described this quality of longsuffering as God's grace "elasticated." It is the stretching out of his grace and mercy toward us over a period of "long continued disobedience."[1]

Someone might say, perhaps in jest, "patience is my middle name," but with God, it literally is. God's patience appears somewhere in the middle of the list of attributes that make up the explanation of his name to Moses: "The LORD, the LORD, a God merciful and gracious, *slow to anger*, and abounding in steadfast love and faithfulness, keeping steadfast love for the thousandth generation, forgiving iniquity and transgression and sin" (Exod 34:6–7).

This same formula is quoted and applied to different contexts throughout the Hebrew Bible. Israel refuses to enter the land and Moses intercedes, reminding God that he is merciful, gracious, and slow to anger (Num 14:18). Then, this very incident is cited by Nehemiah as the people assemble for a day of national fasting and repentance. He reminds them all that God is "ready to forgive, gracious, and merciful, *slow to anger* and abounding in steadfast love" (Neh 9:17). In the Psalms unnamed enemies surround the psalmist. He reminds God of his name: "You, O LORD, are a God merciful and gracious, *slow to anger* and abounding in steadfast love and faithfulness," and, on that basis pleads with God to turn toward

---

1. Berkhof, *Systematic Theology*, 72.

him and "be gracious" to him (Ps 86:15–16). As part of celebrating all aspects of God's goodness and compassion, his longsuffering is again listed in Psalms 103:8 and 145:8. Joel also recites the formula as part of a plea to the people of Judah, in the wake of an ominous plague of locusts, to repent before the day of the LORD brings judgment (Joel 2:13). Jonah complains to God in response to God having relented of judging Nineveh. Such, he felt, was absolutely typical of God: "for I knew that you are a gracious God and merciful, *slow to anger*, and abounding in steadfast love, and ready to relent from punishing" (Jonah 4:2).

In all these passages, the Hebrew underlying "slow to anger" is two words *arech*, "long," and *aph*, "nose"/"nostril"/"face." To be patient is to be long-nosed, or long of face. The nostrils are often pictured as the location of anger, hence, a long nose means that, by the time the air has left the nose, it has cooled, hence words that mean "long-of-nostril" are often rendered as "slow to anger."

This might seem like an odd way to picture patience, but it is no odder than the way we might say that someone has a "very high boiling point." No one literally snorts fiery hot air, and no one literally boils.

In the New Testament, we see the same quality, which in the Greek is *macrothymia*, which is made from *macro*, long and stretched out, and *thymos*, a word that in Classical Greek meant soul or spirit but by the time of the New Testament came to refer to the passions that move the soul, especially anger. *Macrothymia* is the ability to delay retribution, to keep one's anger in abeyance.

This attribute inspired God to wait for people, even the self-righteous, to repent (Rom 2:4), and to delay judgment on those that have got it coming to them (Rom 9:22). God's longsuffering is given as the reason for the delay of Christ's return and the day of judgment (1 Pet 3:20; 2 Pet 3:9, 15).

Our patience comes as a fruit of the Spirit (Gal 5:22) and is how we maintain the unity of the Spirit (Eph 4:2). It goes hand in hand with a readiness always to forgive (Col 3:12). Our patience tends to be the quality that God tests the most. He tests us through short-term provocations and over longer periods when his plans for us have somehow failed to materialize in a timely manner.

God seems willing to bring about any amount of delay in order to give us the best possible opportunity to get ready for what he is about to do. In the letters of Peter, we can see how easy it is to misunderstand God's long-nosedness; his long view of things. We can misunderstand it as inaction, as evidence of apathy or indifference toward us: "The Lord is not slow about his promise, as some think of slowness, but is patient with you, not wanting any to perish, but all to come to repentance" (2 Pet 3:9). This misunderstanding then has a profound effect upon our morality. We start behaving as though he is not watching and does not care: "In the last days scoffers will come, scoffing and indulging their own lusts and saying, 'Where is the promise of his coming? For ever since our ancestors died, all things continue as they were from the beginning of creation!'" (2 Pet 3:3–4).

So, God's patience often tests our patience. We struggle to understand the reason for such long delays—not only the long-delayed return of Christ but the much lesser delays we experience in God answering prayer or doing what we believe he promised he would do. But the reason for the delay is simple: he wants us ready. There may even be some repentance needed.

He also wants to build resilience into us. We had hired a small apartment with a shared outdoor swimming pool on the beautiful Croatian coast near Zadar. In the garden area next to the pool there were some beautifully colored Dalmatian wall lizards, found in that coastal strip and nowhere else in the world. These lived in the lushest, choicest spots, leaving the more adventurous common wall lizards to the more disturbed and arid parts of the garden. My son was in the pool when he suddenly said, "There's a lizard at the bottom of the pool!" He dove down and retrieved it. I assumed it to be long dead. It was a juvenile common wall lizard. To my surprise, when my daughter gave it a rather forceful massage, the tail moved. Soon, it was breathing. We lay it in the sun. Its eyes opened and its head lifted. Then, its front legs came to life, leaving only its back legs that we still not moving and having to be dragged along. Then, someone trod nearby and it scuttled off like any lizard would, everything in full working order. It had shut its whole body down into hibernation mode when it fell in the pool and had now come back to life, recovering from the whole episode in a matter of minutes. It had gone from lying four feet under water in an unheated, chlorinated pool to scuttling off into the bushes in about ten minutes.

The same God who built such remarkable, death-defying resilience into his creatures built us that way too. Have you suffered some knocks? Did you think it was all over? Think of the baby wall lizard, too adventurous for its own good. It was all over for him until my boy fished him out, and the capacity for survival that his creator had endowed him with was all that was needed. He picked up his life just where he left off.

REFLECTION

What is it that is testing your patience right now? Learn the long view and be aware of how, even though you think you might be waiting for God, God might also be waiting for you; waiting for you to be ready for what he is about to give.

Has something floored you? Does it seem like its all over? Remember how God has built you for endurance. You were made for resurrection.

16

Sovereignty

> He rules as king in the most absolute sense of the word, and all things are dependent on Him and subservient to Him.[1]

> With infinite power and infinite wisdom God has, from all eternity past, decided and chosen and determined the course of all events without exception for all eternity to come.[2]

> Were there even one datum of knowledge, however small, unknown to God, His rule would break down at that point. . . . And were God lacking one infinitesimal modicum of power, that lack would end His reign and undo His kingdom.[3]

THESE PASSAGES REMIND US again that all of the attributes are intermingled. God's sovereignty *is* his infinite power, knowledge, and wisdom brought to bear upon our world. This attribute, a little like when I juxtaposed justice and love, represents an apex of both blessing and challenge. To know that God is sovereign in his universe is a source of tremendous comfort to people of faith and is

1. Berkhof, *Systematic Theology*, 76.
2. Buswell, *Systematic Theology of the Christian Religion*, 163.
3. Tozer, *Knowledge of the Holy*, 143.

repeatedly invoked in that way in both Testaments. It is good to know that he is on the throne, and he is not nervous. Yet, because he is on the throne of the universe, the presence of suffering and evil remains a persistent problem to people of faith. God's sovereignty, by definition, entails the absolute freedom of God to act within his universe as and when he pleases: "Our God is in the heavens; he does whatever he pleases" (Ps 115:3). No created being shares in such unqualified and unconstrained freedom. He is entirely free to deal with evil completely and instantly. So, why doesn't he?

A chief characteristic of our world today is pain. All the news headlines are about pain: staggering proliferations of child abuse cases, rising levels of domestic abuse, surprisingly persistent racism and extremism, savage and pointless war, disease on an unprecedented scale, widespread mental ill health, the worst cost-of-living crisis in a generation. Not at any time since World War II have people in the Western world been more profoundly conscious of pain: both their own and that of people all around the world.

There will never be a final answer to this but the word "ultimately" is very useful, much as it can seem like a cop-out. There are two ways in which it can help us to see God being *ultimately* sovereign even while we continue to see evil apparently running amok. Firstly, God's agency in the world operates at an altogether different level to our agency. We are not competing for the same space. Though God can and does intervene forcefully, as we see from the Hebrew Bible, there is no contest between us. He is the being without whom we would have no agency at all. The events we are able to cause could not be caused without him at the source of us. Everything we cause to happen is of an altogether secondary order. God's will and our wills are operating within two different spheres, the one bounded by time and space and the other not.

Human analogies are always limited but we have all been led by someone. We have nearly all had bosses, parents, pastors. So, we know from experience that the good leader tends to be the empowering leader. A good leader, many would say, is someone that creates leadership within and among those being led. The leadership that empowers others is that way not because it is itself weak or limited. People that are truly good at delegating aren't that way because they are weak. Good leadership, it might even be said, consist in award-ing sovereignty to people. A strong leader is strong on a different level to leadership that micromanages or oppresses people. He or she is not competing for the same space as those being led. Good leadership operates in a different space.

The second sense in which God's sovereignty is ultimate is to do with the destination to which it is taking us. At the heart of Christ's kingdom message was the now widely acknowledged "already-not yet" tension. The kingdom had been inaugurated, but not consummated. The reign of God was often pictured by Jesus as being in a state of apparent limitation. He told parables such as the parable of the sower, which, as we saw in chapter 7, portrayed the reign of God as relying on a message that must be embraced by hearts that are ready to hear it. And, of course, in the parable most hearts are very far from ready.

In Romans 9–11, Paul laments the apparent failure of the gos-pel among his fellow Jews. For Paul, the widespread nonacceptance by the Jews of their Messiah potentially calls into question the sov-ereignty of God. He defends God using a number of steps. Firstly, there are no surprises here: the children of Israel always did reject God. This was the lament of all the prophets. God is not caught out (9:30—10:21). Secondly, God's plan all along was to invest in a faithful remnant, an Israel within Israel (11:1–6). Thirdly, the end-game is an even greater plan than might have been obvious before: a plan for a vast ingathering of both gentiles and Jews (11:17–32). Hence, Paul's defense of God's sovereignty is mainly about God's plans for the future, the glorious signs of which were already visible. With the growth of the worldwide church, these signs have become much more apparent since his time of writing.

For meditation, here is a sample of passages celebrating the divine sovereignty:

> Yours, O Lord, are the greatness, the power, the glory,
> the victory, and the majesty; for all that is in the heavens
> and on the earth is yours; yours is the kingdom, O Lord,
> and you are exalted as head above all. Riches and honor
> come from you, and you rule over all. In your hand are

power and might; and it is in your hand to make great
and to give strength to all. (1 Chr 29:11–12)

O LORD, God of our ancestors, are you not God in heav-
en? Do you not rule over all the kingdoms of the nations?
In your hand are power and might, so that no one is able
to withstand you. (2 Chr 20:6)

We know that all things work together for good for those
who love God, who are called according to his purpose.
(Rom 8:28)

He who is the blessed and only Sovereign, the King of
kings and Lord of lords. It is he alone who has immor-
tality and dwells in unapproachable light, whom no one
has ever seen or can see; to him be honor and eternal
dominion. Amen. (1 Tim 6:15–16)

So, how do we respond? Our response to God's sovereignty
has been clarified by Christ's resurrection, ascension, and heavenly
reign: "Therefore let the entire house of Israel know with certainty
that God has made him both Lord and Messiah, this Jesus whom
you crucified," announces Peter to the amazed crowds on the Day of
Pentecost. And our response, according to Paul, is to acknowledge
him as Lord. "[God] highly exalted him and gave him the name
that is above every name so that at the name of Jesus every knee
should bend, in heaven and on earth and under the earth, and every
tongue should confess that Jesus Christ is Lord, to the glory of God
the Father" (Phil 2:9–11). James Hudson Taylor was right: "Christ
is either Lord of all, or is not Lord at all."[4]

I was getting on a bit in my estimation. I was in my early thir-
ties and there was still no love on the horizon. My brother was married at twenty-four and my sister married younger still, but I was
on the shelf. I was perplexed. Sometimes it even seemed as if God
was being cruel, toying with me. He seemed to send my way, once
in a while, a girl that seemed ideal for me. In some cases, I felt that
I was profoundly in love. Alas, it would always end up being an

4 Steer, *Hudson Taylor*, 34.

unrequited love. I was always on the receiving end of the dreaded "Can we just be friends?" And I made each episode drag on for years because I refused to give up hope. I kept praying that the girl would change her mind. After the last episode I had, once again, reluctantly admitted defeat. This time I knew I had to find a way for my battered faith to survive. My self-esteem, too, was in tatters but that could wait. I just needed to find a way to go on believing. I said to him, "Even if nothing good ever comes of anything ever again. Even if you *never* answer any prayers of mine, even if you *never* come through for me, still I will follow you."

I still don't profess to understand all those disappointments but, suffice to say, within just a few months, God did come through for me. I am now happily married with three beautiful children.

God has a plan, the plan is glorious, and the plan will work.

REFLECTION

What are the pressure points in your life where you find it difficult to acknowledge Jesus as Lord or to trust in God's sovereignty? Sometimes it helps if we do something with our bodies. Philippians 2:11 speaks of every knee one day bending to Christ's lordship. Even through pain we bow. Even in tears we kneel, awaiting a fuller understanding of his will.

17

Power

The medieval theologian Thomas Aquinas would distinguish between the absolute power of God (this is, everything he *could* do) and the ordained power of God (everything he *does* in fact do). Scripture seems especially keen to point out that God *can* do absolutely anything—apart from lie, change, sin, or deny himself.

God's *absolute* potency is often described negatively: there is nothing *too hard* for God, or *impossible* for him. These negative statements seem to be used of the miraculous conceptions in the wombs of Sarah and then of Mary (Gen 18:14; Luke 1:37), and remarkable acts of redemption (salvation for exiled Israel [Jer 32:17, 27] or *even* for a rich person [Matt 19:26]).

The positive version of the same truth, that anything *is* possible appears in the context of the man with a tormented and demonized boy (Mark 9:23) and God's absolute power is described both *negatively and positively* by Job as God reveals himself to him: "I know that you can do all things, and that no purpose of yours can be thwarted" (Job 42:2). God can do everything, *and* nothing is impossible for him.

The *ordained* power of God, in contrast to the abstractions of the *absolute* power of God, includes all the things that God has decreed to carry out or has in fact already achieved. These include the most outstanding events in all human history. They are the supreme demonstrations of his super-exalted position over all other gods.

For ancient Israel, the supreme act of power was the exodus. For the church, it is the resurrection of Christ. The resurrection is so remarkable it warrants a tumbling cascade of superlatives. It shows

> the immeasurable greatness of his power for us who believe, according to the working of his great power. God put this power to work in Christ when he raised him from the dead and seated him at his right hand in the heavenly places. (Eph 1:19–20)

An effective prayer life seems to derive its best energies from dwelling in that hinterland between the absolute power of God and the ordained power of God. Faith dwells upon all that God *could* do and seeks to persuade God that there is something he *should* do. Our convictions about all that God should do are fed by history. We remember what God has in fact done and ask him to do it again. And, prayer is answered when God, always amazingly, does in fact do it. He joyfully yields to our arm-twisting citations of history and lovingly stoops to our castigations of his slowness to act.

Faith and prayer thrive and grow within the reality that God "is able to do exceedingly abundantly above all that we ask or think" (Eph 3:20). This means that prayer is fed by the prophetic imagination, by visionary thoughts, by pictures of what *could* be. It experiments with voicing these hopes in the ears of God and rejoices when God answers. And, whenever he answers, it always exceeds what we imagined; it is always somehow better than what we asked or thought.

What God has in fact done then gets added to the bank of what we know of his ordained power, the bank of what he has in fact done. Resting atop is the supreme act (the resurrection of Christ) below which we place all lesser acts (everything that God has ever done in answer to our prayers). Like the psalmist did when he was feeling discouraged, we remember his mighty acts (e.g., Ps 42:6), and we are emboldened once again to occupy that hinterland of prophetic imagination and see if God will do yet more impossible things.

At this point I am going to refrain from giving any of my own stories of God's power working the impossible for me. Many of us have been overexposed to "testimonies." These range from the spectacular ("God got me out of a wheelchair") to the banal ("God gave me a parking space"), but one thing they seldom are is sensitive. Our churches are full of pain. They are full of people who have resolved to find God within their situation rather than longing for some spectacular deliverance.

I would encourage you to remember your own breakthroughs, however small or great these may have been.

REFLECTION

Remember what God has done. Give thanks for all the most remarkable answers to prayer you have ever experienced. Then, try asking for what you dream of.

<h1 style="text-align:center">18</h1>

Attending to Beauty

I WANT TO RETURN to the subject of beauty.

As seems clear, there are ways of encountering the attributes of God relatively directly, during wonderful moments, those experiences of the numinous. Much as we try to keep our connection with God live all the time, it sometimes dies. We lose connectivity surprisingly easily when life gangs up on us. We are mostly *not* like the esteemed Brother Lawrence who, by practicing familiar conversation with God over many years, ended up in a state of unbroken communion. He even said, "I no longer believe, but see."[1] We would probably all love to be where he was: in a place of such immediate and vivid experience of the glory of God that we don't need to "faith it" anymore.

This, I think is where beauty comes in. If we are on the lookout for it, beauty will save us from ourselves and connect us to God again.

In sacramental traditions, such as Roman Catholicism, Eastern Orthodoxy, or High Anglicanism, there has always been, right at the center of the worship of the gathered church, an element of drama, of nonverbal communication, of sign and symbol: a liturgical art-form that retells an ancient story. In non-sacramental traditions, the Bible takes center stage. For many within these traditions, there has only ever been one way of bringing an intelligible message

1. Brother Lawrence, *The Practice of the Presence of God*, 54.

to the world, and that is to explain and declare the words that lie on the Bible's pages. Anything nonverbal is purely for illustrative or decorative purposes.

One of the reasons why I laid down my brief career as an artist was the frustration I had that I could not, in any direct or unambiguous way, preach the gospel through my paintings. I had completely taken on board the assumptions of my church tradition that the straightforward verbal communication of the Word of God was the best way of making a real impact. I genuinely shared the sentiment that it would be far easier simply to use words, especially if evangelism was the only legitimate reason for being an artist (and to me it was). So before long I turned my attention to preaching, teaching, and writing, which has all proved fruitful. But what I did not have at my disposal was an alternative, less wordy understanding of how faith could be stimulated. I did not have a sacramental worldview.

A sacrament, according to Augustine, was "an outward sign of an inward grace." And, today, in Roman Catholic thinking, God can be present in anything. He can be present, for example, in a painting, but, building upon the historic deliberations of Hugh of St. Victor and Peter Lombard, Roman Catholicism has refined its definitions a lot since Augustine. A sacrament cannot be simply anything (though, potentially, anything at all could have a sort of sacramental power, but of a lesser order). Donald Baillie affirms, "Nothing could be in the special sense a sacrament unless everything were in a basic and general sense sacramental."[2] Yet caution is needed and has been voiced for a long time over what the poet W. H Auden (1907–73) termed "pansacramentalism." He cautioned that to see the universe as a whole as a sacrament is to run the risk of becoming a "pantheist," someone who believes that creation is itself divine: "The pantheist believes that the universe is numinous *as-a-whole*. But a sacramental sign is always some particular aspect of the finite, *this* thing, this act, not the finite-in-general."[3] Hence, Roman Catholicism continues to restrict the sacraments proper to the seven listed by the Fourth Lateran Council.

2. Baillie, *Theology of the Sacraments*, 42.

3. Auden, *The Dyer's Hand*, cited by Eversole, "Art and Sacrament," 393.

However, even though the sacraments as such are narrowly defined, they tell us something more general about the way our spirituality works. There is a general sense in which "the spiritual can be conveyed through the material."[4] Here is Baillie again:

> We must believe that when Christianity took the common elements of water and bread and wine and made sacraments of them, it was because this universe is the sacramental kind of place in which that can fitly happen; because these elements, these creatures of God, do lend themselves to such a use; and because we men and women, who are another sort of God's creatures, do require in our religion such a use of material things and symbolic actions.[5]

To faith, the objects of God's created order—whether these be artistically adapted by humans or not—can be an address from God simply because it is God that made all things. And such things, when humanly adapted, may serve as both an expression of faith and as the means of awakening faith. Such things are among the many means that God employs to win people over to himself.

Such things are really extensions of the incarnation, says Baillie.[6] Paul Tillich was bold enough to describe the sacramental reality as "nothing else than some reality becoming the bearer of the holy in a special way under special circumstances."[7] A sacrament is the "space-time of the sacred."[8] A sacramental worldview, then, rejects the idea that there can ever be a hard boundary between the material and the spiritual. Matter and spirit are, according to this vision of life, "deeply interfused."[9] Because of this, art is a "means and vehicle of worship" rather than "decoration" or "bait."[10]

4. Sherry, *Spirit and Beauty*, 139.

5. Baillie, *Theology of the Sacraments*, 44. Baillie also cites Jesus himself: "Consider the lilies . . ." (Matt 6:28–30); Baillie, *Theology of the Sacraments*, 46.

6. Baillie, *Theology of the Sacraments*, 61.

7. Tillich, *Theology of Culture*, 72.

8. Eversole, "Art and Sacrament," 394.

9. Hunter, "Arts in Relation to the Sacraments," 473.

10. Hunter, "Arts in Relation to the Sacraments," 473.

Salvador Dali ranks as one of the most imaginative artists ever to have lived. Having, during his surrealist period, explored subconscious realms via his dreamscapes, his art and life underwent a radical and change during the 1950s following his conversion to Catholicism. Four paintings from this period are noteworthy: *The Madonna of Port Lligat* (1950), *Christ of St. John of the Cross* (1951), *Nuclear Cross* (1952), and, most famous, his *Sacrament of the Last Supper* (1955).

Fundamentally, Dali believed that the very process of painting itself mediated God's grace. The finished painting communicated grace to the viewer via its atoms and molecules: "Instead of wine and bread it was a transubstantiation of matter in oil, thinner, and image that communicated sacramental power and real presence."[11] He was fascinated by the question of how material objects could in some way carry the divine, a fascination very much fed by the very high value placed on sacramental objects, such as relics, by Spanish Catholicism.[12] He liked to blur the lines between the material and immaterial. There are floating, levitating figures that do not seem fully material, and the use of geometric forms combined with attentiveness to perfect, divine proportion. In this way, all was infused with meaning: the composition, the forms, painting style: everything. He placed particular importance upon his *Sacrament of the Last Supper* as the painting that best achieved his aims: "In that picture can be read all of my cosmology, the union of time and space which is the secret of God."[13] He claimed that "each picture is a Mass in which I distribute the Eucharist of a knowledge."[14]

A significant part of Christian art's sacramental function is its dialogue between the immanent and the transcendent, between the earthly and the heavenly, between the already and the not yet, between suffering and glory, between weakness and sin and God's redemption and love. When Christian art achieves this dialogue

11. Myhre, "Painting as Sacrament," 26.

12. Myhre, "Painting as Sacrament," 26.

13. Myhre, "Painting as Sacrament," 28, citing Dali in Andre Parinaud, *The Unspeakable Confession of Salvador Dali* (New York: Morrow, 1976), 226.

14. Myhre, "Painting as Sacrament," 28, citing Dali in Robert Descharnes, *Salvador Dali* (New York: Abrams, 1976), 246.

successfully, it becomes truly great art. In fact, it could even be said that all great art is great precisely because of this kind of greatness. Great art displays a breadth of vision that can bring into conversation divergent aspects of our reality. It elevates the soul while describing harsh or banal realities.

As the Dutch still-life artists made clear, it is a dialogue that can take place with the most mundane of scenes. Stanley Spencer is another example from the world of painting. Arguably, it is precisely in working with the everyday, the humdrum, the routine of life that the greatest potential exists to articulate this heaven-and-earth dialogue in a most striking way. Describing one of his famous Resurrection paintings, Spencer explains:

> Everything has a sort of double meaning for me, there's the ordinary everyday meaning of things, and the imaginary meaning about it all, and I wanted to bring these things together, and in this first big Resurrection of mine you have a good example of this sort of thing.[15]

God's common grace is such that we must always be ready to appreciate the work of those without an obvious faith. For instance, Mark Greene, CEO of the London Institute for Contemporary Christianity, praises the "breathtaking originality"[16] of the guitar solo in Jimi Hendrix's version of "All Along the Watchtower." It is tremendously inventive: possibly the most eccentric of guitar solos ever played. It does not stick to any of the usual formulae and is more about melody than rapid-playing prowess. And it seems to achieve transcendence. It takes you "up there."

To gaze upon the beauty of God involves us in an encounter. This much is obvious, but that encounter can either be relatively direct—touching our senses and emotions with an awareness of the proximity of the divine presence—or more mediated; it can take place through the beautiful creations of our world, whether fashioned by humans or not. With our doors of perception cleansed[17]

15. Stanley Spencer, original source unknown; see https://www.thehistoryofart.org/stanley-spencer/quotes/.

16. Greene, *Great Divide*, 15.

17. I'm alluding to William Blake: "If the doors of perception were cleansed

even a vacation somewhere beautiful can become a sacred meeting or a divine Word to us, not just a refreshing break. And, going back to music, Jeremy Begbie suggests that there might even be something within the musicality of some worship songs, the cadences themselves, that speak to us of homecoming and safety, before we even think about the words.

REFLECTION

My point in this chapter has been that the world is rigged in such a way that, because everything participates in the divine, there is the potential to find God in anything. From God's viewpoint there is no secular. From his standpoint there is nothing wholly natural and nothing wholly supernatural.

Looking for beauty portals is about attending to the world around us in a way that expects it to speak of its creator.

May our eyes be opened.

---

everything would appear to man as it is, Infinite. For man has closed himself up, till he sees all things through narrow chinks of his cavern" (*Marriage of Heaven and Hell*, 26).

Conclusion

So, WE HAVE SEEN that God is the uncaused cause and fountain-head of all that is. We have seen that he is, therefore, not bound by time or space, yet can inhabit both. He cannot be improved upon, therefore does not change, and he is the one and only, the I AM, the God-who-is, who alone is worthy of our worship. Because he is everywhere his knowledge is absolute and unacquired and his wisdom is matchless. Because he does not change, his integrity is flawless: he is truth itself. Because he is exalted, he has never been in any way sullied by this earth and its sin and evil and is therefore the only one absolutely qualified to be Judge of the living and the dead. Yet, for all the terror that his righteousness and justice might arouse, he is so full of love as to be referred to as love itself. The love does not cancel out the justice, nor the justice cancel out the love. This love is expressed in his bountiful kindness toward all he has made, his astonishing grace toward the undeserving, his unfailing mercy toward us, and his limitless patience with us. Finally, and without quashing the free will he has given us, he reigns as King in the most absolute sense imaginable and can do the most unimaginable things: things that seem impossible to us.

This is the God and Father of our Lord Jesus Christ, the Son of the living God, and the Spirit, the Lord and Life-Giver: one divine essence in three distinct persons: the Father sending, the Son and Spirit sent. Sent to do what? Sent to seek us out, make us part of his mission and finally to take us home where we can forever gaze upon the beauty of God.

Bibliography

Anselm. *Proslogion*. Translated by Sidney Norton Deane. LaSalle, IL: Open Court, 1903. http://www.logoslibrary.org/anselm/proslogion/.

Aquinas, Thomas. *Summa Theologiae*. https://www.newadvent.org/summa/.

Baillie, John. *Theology of the Sacraments*. London: Faber & Faber, 1957.

Balthasar, Hans Urs von. *Theological Aesthetics: Glory of the Lord*. Vol. 2, *Studies in Theological Styles: Clerical Style*. Translated by Andrew Louth, Francis McDonagh, and Brian McNeill. Edinburgh: T. & T. Clark, 1984.

Barth, Karl. *Dogmatics in Outline*. Translated by G. T. Thomson. London: HarperCollins, 1949.

Begbie, Jeremy. *Voicing Creation's Praise: Towards a Theology of the Arts*. Edinburgh: T. & T. Clark, 1991.

Berkhof, Louis. *Systematic Theology*. Edinburgh: Banner of Truth, 1958.

Blake, William. *The Marriage of Heaven and Hell*. Boston: John W. Luce, 1906.

Brother Lawrence. *The Practice of the Presence of God*. London: Hodder & Stoughton, 1997.

Buswell, James. *A Systematic Theology of the Christian Religion*. Vol. 1. Grand Rapids: Zondervan, 1962.

Critchley, Simon, and William Schroeder, eds. *Blackwell Companion to Continental Philosophy*. Oxford: Blackwell, 1998.

Daly, Jason. "We Haven't Been Zapped Out of Existence Yet, So Other Dimensions Are Probably Super Tiny." *Smithsonian Magazine*, October 8, 2018. https://www.smithsonianmag.com/smart-news/our-continued-existence-means-other-dimensions-are-probably-super-tiny-180970487.

De Gruchy, John. *Christianity, Art and Transformation*. Cambridge: Cambridge University Press, 2001.

De Lubac, Henri. *The Drama of Atheist Humanism*. San Francisco: Ignatius, 1995.

Descartes, René. *Meditations*. Translated and edited by Arthur Wollaston. In *Descartes Discourse on Method and Other Writings*. London: Penguin, 1960.

Dostoyevsky, Fyodor. *The Idiot*. Ware, UK: Wordsworth, 1996.

Dyrness, William. *Visual Faith: Art, Theology, and Worship in Dialogue*. Grand Rapids: Baker, 2001.

Edwards, Jonathan. *The Nature of True Virtue*. In *The Works of Jonathan Edwards A.M.*, vol. 1, edited by E. Hickman. London: William Ball, 1839.

Epstein, I., trans. *The Babylonian Talmud*. 18 vols. London: Soncino, 1935–48.

Eversole, Finley. "Art and Sacrament: Protestant Sacramentalism Has Something to Learn from the Symbolism Found in Contemporary Artistic Creation." *Christian Century*, March 25, 1964, 393–96.

Greene, Mark. *The Great Divide*. London: LICC, 2010.

Gustafsson, Daniel. "The Beauty of Christian Art." *Forum Philosophicum* 17.2 (2012) 175–96.

Hart, David Bentley. *The Beauty of the Infinite: The Aesthetics of Christian Truth*. Grand Rapids: Eerdmans, 2003.

Hunter, Leslie. "The Arts in Relation to the Sacraments." *Modern Churchman* 16.6–8 (1926) 471–78.

Lewis, C. S. *The Screwtape Letters*. San Francisco: HarperCollins, 1996.

Liddel, H. G., and R. Scott. *A Greek-English Lexicon*. Abridged. Oxford: Clarendon, 1994.

Myhre, Paul. "Painting as Sacrament: A Search for Dali's Sacramental Imagination." *ARTS: The Arts in Religious and Theological Studies* (2006) 24–29.

NASA. "Is There Life on Other Planets?" *Exoplanet Exploration: Planets Beyond Our Solar System*. https://exoplanets.nasa.gov/faq/5/is-there-life-on-other-planets.

Otto, Rudolf. *The Idea of the Holy*. Rev. ed. London: Oxford University Press, 1931.

Packer, J. I. *Knowing God*. London: Hodder & Stoughton, 1993.

Packham, Chris, and Megan McCubbin. *Back to Nature: How to Love Life—and Save It*. London: Two Roads, 2020.

Plato. *The Works of Plato*. Translated by Benjamin Jowett. London: Random House, 1977.

Prothro, James. *Both Judge and Justifier: Biblical Legal Language and the Act of Justifying in Paul*. Tübingen: Mohr Siebeck, 2018.

Ryken, Philip. *Art for God's Sake*. Phillipsburg: P. & R., 2006.

Scruton, Roger. *Beauty*. Oxford: Oxford University Press, 2009.

Sherry, Patrick. *Spirit and Beauty: An Introduction to Theological Aesthetics*. Oxford: Clarendon, 1992.

Spurgeon, Charles. *Spurgeon's Sermons*. Vol. 22, *1876*. https://ccel.org/ccel/spurgeon/sermons22/sermons22.

Steer, Roger. *Hudson Taylor: Lessons in Discipleship*. Crowborough, UK: Monarch, 1995.

Thiessen, Henry. *Lectures in Systematic Theology*. Grand Rapids: Eerdmans, 1979.

Thomas, Rick. "Addiction Defined Is a Worship Disorder, Pt. 2" *Life over Coffee* (blog). https://lifeovercoffee.com/addiction-defined-worship-disorder-pt-2.

Tillich, Paul. *Theology of Culture*. Edited by Robert Kimball. Oxford: Oxford University Press, 1959.

BIBLIOGRAPHY

Treier, Daniel, Mark Husbands, and Roger Lundin, eds. *The Beauty of God*. Downers Grove, IL: InterVarsity, 2007.
Tozer, A. W. *The Knowledge of the Holy*. Eastbourne, UK: Kingsway, 1989.
Weiser, Artur. *The Psalms*. London: SCM, 1962.

9 781666 750676